San Francisco Theatre Research: The Starks
; the Bakers ; the Chapmans / Lawrence
Estavan, Editor

SAN FRANCISCO THEATRE RESEARCH

MONOGRAPHS:

THE STARKS

THE BAKERS

THE CHAPLANS

VOLUME THREE

FIRST
SERIES

Abstract from
WPA Project 8386
O.P. 465-03-286

SAN FRANCISCO, CALIFORNIA
1938

These volumes have been prepared:

VOLUME I.
INTRODUCTION TO THE SERIES
San Francisco's Earliest Entertainers:
STEPHEN C. MASSETT
JOSEPH A. ROWE

VOLUME II.
Pioneer Impresarios:
TOM MAGUIRE
DOC ROBINSON
M. B. LEAVITT

VOLUME III.
Famous Early Families:
THE STARKS
THE BAKERS
THE CHAPMANS

VOLUME IV.
The Booth Family:
JUNIUS BRUTUS BOOTH SR.
JUNIUS BRUTUS BOOTH JR.
EDWIN BOOTH

VOLUME V.
LOLA MONTEZ
LOTTA CRABTREE
IDAH ISAACS MENKEN

VOLUME VI - No. 1
Foreign Theatres
ITALIAN
FRENCH
GERMAN

VOLUME VII.
THE HISTORY OF OPERA IN
SAN FRANCISCO

Other volumes in preparation
will include, among other
subjects:

Pioneer Prima Donnas:
ELIZA BISCACCIANTI
ANNA BISHOP
CATHERINE HAYES
LUISA TETRAZZINI

SYBIL SANDERSON
EMMA NEVADA
MAUDE FAY

Other Actors and Actresses:
SOPHIE EDWIN
MRS. JUDAH
ADELAIDE NEILSON
CATHERINE SINCLAIR
JAMES E. MURDOCH
JOHN MCCULLOUGH
FRANK MAYO
GOUGENHEIM SISTERS
LAURA KEENE
MARY ANDERSON
EDWIN FORREST
CHARLES WHEATLEIGH
JAMES HENRY VINSON
JOSEPH JEFFERSON
EDWIN ADAMS
SAMUEL PIERCEY
J. H. MCCABE
WALTER M. LEMAN
ANNA QUINN
SUE ROBINSON
ALICE KINGSBURY
WEBB & WORRELL SISTERS
MAUDE ADAMS
THE BATEMANS
MAXINE ELLIOTT
NANCE O'NEILL
EMILIE MELVILLE
BLANCHE BATES
DAVID WARFIELD
DE WOLF HOPPER
HOLBROOK BLINN
LAURA HOPE CREWS
DAVID BELASCO
OLIVER MOROSCO
ROLLO PETERS

Volumes on period history:
THEATRE BUILDINGS

MINSTRELSY

BURLESQUE

PERIOD COSTUMES

×792.079
Un3 3

462909

San Francisco Theatre Research

Vol. 3

MONOGRAPHS

VI: THE STARKS

VII: THE BAKERS

VIII: THE CHAPMANS

Lawrence Estavan, Editor. San Francisco, July 1938
Monographs VI, VII and VIII from Theatre Research
W.P.A. Project 8386, O.P. 465-03-3-286

TABLE OF CONTENTS

THE STARKS

(James Stark 1819-1875) (Mrs. Stark 1813-1898)

TABLE OF CONTENTS (Cont.)

THE BAKERS

(John Lewis Baker, 1825-1873) (Mrs Baker, 1822-1887)

THE CHAPMANS

(For dates, see Family Tree on Chapmans)

TABLE OF CONTENTS (cont.)

J A M E S   S T A R K

1819-1875

MRS. JAMES STARK

(1823 - 1898)

THE STARKS

Pioneer Tragedians

It would hardly be expected that the miners of
'50, struggling fiercely with earth and rock all day, drink-
ing and gambling wildly all night, would take an especial delight in the blank verse of Shakespeare declaimed across the
footlights, or in the brittle dialogue of English comedies of
manners. But this was one of the strangest phenomena of life
in San Francisco during the early days. Then drama was amaz-
ingly popular. Not only did San Francisco find in the theatre
an escape from its rough, coarse, turbulent existence but perhaps also an articulate expression that was its daily life.

That untutored genius, Tom Maguire, had an in-
stinct for gauging public taste in the theatre. In building
his Jenny Lind Theatre he decided on the proper atmosphere.
He constructed the theatre lavishly, with elaborate and opulent
equipment and settings. He decided that the public was eager
to see Shakespeare and the English comedies performed skillfully. Accordingly, on November 4, 1850 he opened the Jenny
Lind under the management of James Stark, a young, ambitious
tragedian, and Mrs. Kirby, a minor actress on-stage with a

*See Volume 2 of this series.

facility for off-stage melodrama.

James Stark was born at Windsor, Canada, August 16, 1819. The girl who was to become his wife and partner-actor-manager was born in 1813, but research so far has not revealed the exact day and month of her birth nor her maiden name except that her first name was Sarah. When Stark first met her she had been married twice; first to J. Hudson Kirby, whose name she had retained on the stage, and second, to a man whose name is variously recorded as Wingard, Wingered or Wingate.*

The first husband, Kirby, was a young English actor who had had great popular success in New York, specializing in deathbed agonies. He had abundant rehearsal for his own abrupt end, at the age of 29, in London. This was in 1848. Shortly afterwards Mrs. Kirby returned to America and married Wingate. Together they came to San Francisco in January,1850.

MRS. STARK'S DEBUT

The next month Mrs. Wingate made her debut in Rowe's Amphitheatre, playing Pauline in the Lady of Lyons, and ending her season on March 11. When she opened the Jenny Lind with James Stark on November 4, she still retained the name of Kirby for stage purposes. In fact she had very little time to get used to the other name, for less than two weeks later Mr. Wingate fell from a horse and died. Regretfully the season was closed until November 25 to grant the widow

*The Harvard University Theatre Library prefers Wingate.

her period of mourning. Six months later she married Stark.

Mrs. Kirby Wingate Stark was, according to all reports, very much devoted to her husbands. Their early deaths were a reflection of the violence of the times. It was quite common for theatres suddenly to go up in smoke, or actors' lives to be snuffed out abruptly by accidents, quarrels, suicides.

A TRAGIC EPISODE

During January 1851, the season at the Jenny Lind was again interrupted, this time by a suicide. Mrs. John Hambleton, a member of the company, poisoned herself one afternoon, and the whole story was blurted out to the news-papers. It was a drama strikingly reminiscent of I Pagliacci which involved almost the entire company and in which Mr. Hambleton, and Mrs. Kirby competed for the role of chief vil-lain. The unhappy heroine was of course the love-striken Mrs. Hableton. The ardent lover was a Mr. Coad; the jealous husband, Mr. Hambleton. There was the orthodox triangle, the standard denouement, the confrontation of the guilty pair by the husband, the tragedy. But into the relationship an in-truder had entered, complicating the plot. It was Mrs. Kirby.

In the un-private pages of The Picayune of January 15, the epilogue was enacted. Mr. Hambleton publicly charged Mrs. Kirby with the guilt of the tragedy; it was Mrs. Kirby who had alienated the affections of his wife, instilled the venom, the treachery in the mind of the helpless victim. He absolved Mr. Coad of guilt; to him it was Mrs. Kirby's

"officious counsel" that caused the disaster. The next day Mrs. Kirby indignantly replied, informing the world of Mr. Hambleton's cruelty, giving details of his brutality, and denying any connection with the affair, except as sympathetic confidante of the late Mrs. Hambleton. This charge was endorsed by statements published by Coad and by Mrs Hambleton's friends. The letter concluded with a lofty patriotic note; Mrs. Kirby complained of Hambleton's persecution of her because she was an American actress. She called upon all good Americans to defend her honor as an actress against the attacks of foreigners.

This was a clever move on her part. She had not forgotten the Astor Place riots in New York a few years previously when during a dispute concerning the respective merits of an American actor, Forrest, and an English actor, Macready, several people were killed. The theatre was very close to life in those days, and Shakespeare, opera, the personal lives of actors, the emotions of the audience were intermingled. The highly colored, agitated life of a Mrs. Kirby-Stark was characteristic of those days, a dramatic tempest fusing together the theatre and life.

JAMES STARK'S EARLY CAREER

James Stark was a quieter personality. Most of his life was limited to the stage, but he too had reasons for remembering the Astor Place riot. It was Macready who had been his teacher; and for many years he remained the faithful disciple

of the English star.

Before he went on the stage Stark was a carpenter in Nova Scotia. He was strongly attracted to the theatre and for this reason emigrated to Boston where there were greater opportunities for study of acting. He discovered a patron in a fellow-member of a dramatic club, an Abbott Lawrence, who had enthusiasm for Stark's talent and earnestness, persuading him to go to Europe, and financing him for three years of study in London and on the continent.

STARK AS TRAGEDIAN

When James Stark returned to America he was an actor -- but not a finished one. He remained always a student, seeking constantly to perfect himself in his art, and during the years gradually improving in mastery of technique. When he arrived in San Francisco he was preceded by a reputation as a tragedian; he was the first important star to come to San Francisco, a pioneer, making the road easier for the long succession of great actors that were to follow him, creating a taste in the public for the great tragedies of Shakespeare and for good acting.

But he did not plunge directly into Shakespeare: he made his first appearance at the Jenny Lind as Damon in Damon and Pythias. The effect was disappointing; the play did not bring out his talents as a tragedian. It was only in high tragedy that Stark excelled; Damon and Pythias itself was an inferior play, full of rant and fustian. The critic of the

Picayune, (Nov. 5, 1850) also found the makeup to be unexpectedly ludicrous; there was obviously too much wig and too
much beard so that poor Damon seemed to be always on the
verge of toppling over. He found Mrs. Kirby as Hermione to
be effective, despite her illness; and also good points about
the acting of the Hambletons.

CRITICAL ESTIMATE ON OTHELLO

The next night Othello was given. This was not the
first time that Othello had been presented to San Francisco;
a few months before in an unexpectedly serious mood Rowe had
deserted circus and produced Othello in his amphitheatre. But
this one was a finished production, and for the first time
Stark showed San Francisco what he could do: he was in his
element -- and, in The Picayune, Nov. 6, 1850 the critic expressed his appreciation in rather involved phraseology:

> "Mr. Stark's Othello was a masterly and finish-
> ed exhibition of the character. It appeared
> perfectly evident that he is not a copyist or
> imitator of any model actor; but that he stud-
> ies with close application of mind the charac-
> ter he undertakes to represent, and he seems to
> us in this instance to have succeeded admirably
> well in placing his mind in the attitude and
> frame of the great author of the tragedy in
> taking his conception of the character and
> bearing of the Moor. He does not, therefore,
> show us Macready's Othello, or Forrest's but
> Shakespeare's, and we have never seen what in
> our judgment, was a truer or more forcible pre-
> sentation."

Stark, in fact, had so deeply entered into the
character and was so carried away by the spirit of the play
that in the last act he stabbed himself very painfully.

Now Mr. Stark was severely wounded; Mrs. Kirby was
still suffering from her illness; the Hambletons were simmer-
ing with love and jealousy. But the show must go on.   And
the next night they played in another tragedy, the Roman
tragedy of Sheridan Knowles, Virginius, with Stark in the
title role, and Mrs. Kirby as Virginia: "natural, graceful
and eloquent."*

REVIVAL OF THE WIFE

At times during this first season in San Francisco
Stark considered that he was aiming too high and that he
should make occasional concessions to popular taste. Tragedies were interspersed with short light pieces, and even at
this early date revivals were given.   Standards of taste are
based upon habit: the public has a fondness for the familiar:
thus, (on Nov. 8, 1850) Stark, Mrs. Kirby and the Hambletons
revived that old favorite, The Wife, the first play produced
in San Francisco. With this off his mind, Stark the next day
introduced Shylock to San Francisco. And for the next evening he became Hamlet.   The miners were getting some pretty
stiff doses of Shakespeare and they were enjoying it. They
crowded the Jenny Lind night after night listening intently
to the speeches applauding the acting apparently undistracted
by the irrelevant music from Maguire's saloon below.

The afterpiece must occasionally have seemed an an-
ticlimax.   Thus the Alta California (Dec. 19, 1850) having

* Picayune, Nov. 7, 1850.

exhausted all the superlatives in connection with "Hamlet, the greatest play of the greatest poet of all times, and decidedly J. Stark's best representation" -- lamely concludes: "the whole to conclude with State Secrets."

STARK AS HAMLET, RICHELIEU

Hamlet was so far Stark's performance; his bringing Hamlet to San Francisco for the first time entitles him officially to the designation of "pioneer tragedian." Hamlet was proficiently done, but because there have been so many very famous Hamlets in America his particular version is forgotten. However, there were certain characterizations that were particularly fine. Walter Leman (Memories of An Old Actor, p. 247) singles out two worthy of memory: Cardinal Richelieu in Richelieu, and Beverly in The Gamester. The Alta agreed with this verdict, on Dec. 23 it said:

> "The character of Richelieu is, we think, one of Stark's best impersonations, although he does not so consider it. His conception of the character is true and his delineation of the various and rapid changes which the wily strong-willed politician exhibits in his manner, as hope or danger or triumph or patriotism by turns find expression and utterance, is artistic, truthful and effective."

CRITICAL ESTIMATE OF MRS. STARK

And Mrs. Kirby was likewise excellent:

"As Julie de Mortimer Mrs. Kirby has heretofore won worthily the admiration of the admirers of this fine drama. The affectionate and confiding ward of the old Cardinal, a daughter by all the ties of gratitude and dependence, obedient

yet persuasive and eloquent in her pleadings
for the man she loves; in fine the exhibition
of those peculiarly female characteristics of
heart, manner, and expression, which the character of Julie requires, find in Mrs. Kirby's
impersonation a very correct expression."

The year 1850 came to an end with two other famous
plays: Pizarro and Venice Preserved. Then Mr. Stark and Mrs.
Kirby paid a brief visit to Stockton, where they had great
success. On Feb. 29, 1851 they were back again in San Francisco and Mrs. Kirby deserted the now already established
team of Stark and Kirby to give a solo performance; she appeared as Pauline in the Lady of Lyons, which had been her
first role in San Francisco a year previously.

STARK'S SUCCESS AS IAGO

The season was concluded during March with a few
performances of Othello. It had been given before but this
was a special Othello, for this time Stark did not play the
jealous Moor, but the villain, Iago. It had been discovered
that he displayed unexpected ability as Iago, much more than
he had previously exhibited as Othello. His performance as
Iago in Stockton had caused much comment, and the anticipa-
tion was great. "We are lead to the expectation," said the
Alta of March 7, "of seeing the best piece of acting ever
given on these shores."

They were not disappointed, and his Iago as one of
his admittedly greatest interpretations ended the season at
the Jenny Lind. With Mrs. Kirby he went to Sacramento, and

when they returned in June the old Jenny Lind was no longer;
during their absence a month previously it had been destroyed
by fire.

SHAKESPEARE AND THE MINERS

Thus with characteristic abruptness ended the first
phase of the Starks career in San Francisco.   It had been an
uncertain and exciting period, full of unexpected catastro-
phes. But they were pioneer actors and their function was to
experience all the hardships, so as to make the way easier
for their followers.   They had successfully launched Shakespeare in San Francisco; they had succeeded in getting crowded houses every night, not by playing down to the audience
but by raising it to their level. Night after night they had
hurled full versions of Shakespeare at the miners and the
miners had clamored for more.   For the first time San Francisco heard Hamlet, Macbeth, King Lear, Much Ado about Nothing, The Merchant of Venice, The Taming of the Shrew.
Important comedies, such as Sheridan's The Rivals, were also
introduced to San Francisco, but it was in tragedy that Stark
was most effective.

That crowded season at the old Jenny Lind practically exhausted the entire repertoires. The seasons that followed were built on the foundation already established during
this first season, perfecting the interpretations of these
roles.

THE STARKS MANAGE THE JENNY LIND

In Sacramento Stark and Mrs. Kirby repeated their San Francisco success.   They were familiar to the Sacramento public; indeed before coming to San Francisco they had played a long season at the Tehama Theatre, of which they were the lessees.   Now while they were playing in Sacramento the San Francisco public was clamoring for their return; its thirst for Shakespeare had evidently been unsated.   Willingly they returned in June, only to be greeted by the ashes of their theatre.   For Maguire this was a slight inconvenience; he immediately proceeded to rebuild the Jenny Lind for them.   On June 13, 1851 Mr. Stark and Mrs. Kirby took over the management of this new theatre.   The next day they were married in Sacramento.

Mrs. Kirby now became Mrs. Stark, on and off stage. For the rest of her husband's career she followed him from theatre to theatre, content to play any supporting role in his company.   Together they formed an acting family, an institution fairly common in those early days -- as it still is in continental Europe where the company is a close group composed of the patriarchal capo comiche, the wife and children, sons and daughters-in-law. Mrs. Stark despite her overwhelming personality was sensibly able to subordinate herself to her more brilliant husband.

BURNING OF THE JENNY LIND

This marriage, however successful from this point

of view, started out very inauspiciously. A week after their
wedding, Sacramento, docilely following the trend of her
sister city of San Francisco, had a mighty conflagration and
in it their theatre, the Tehama, was destroyed. And the next
day San Francisco not to be outdone had her fire and the second Jenny Lind was burned to the ground.

The Starks were now homeless -- a miserable beginning for their married life; all summer they wandered about
San Francisco looking around for some kind of stage. But the
fire that consumed the Jenny Lind had also destroyed all the
other available theatres: the Dramatic Museum, the Adelphi,
as well as lesser houses; and Maguire was becoming more wary.
It was true that he had luck in gauging the public tendencies
but he had no way of determining when a fire might suddenly
occur and upset his plans. So he waited. . . . Meanwhile the
Starks' funds were diminishing. Although they had had successful seasons in both cities, the Starks like most actors
of history reckless, generous, and improvident could not
cling to the money they earned.

But the public of San Francisco, especially in
those days, was always eager to lend a helping hand. To com-
pensate for their loss of the Tehama Theatre a huge benefit
was staged on August 22 at the Adelphi. And now their luck
seemed to be changing. Two weeks later they were engaged at
this new little theatre. From there they went to Robinson's
new theatre, the American, on October 20.

THE THEATRE SINKS

The American engagement went off to a bad start.
Here again disaster seemed to be dogging the steps of the
Stark family. They had been pursued from theatre to theatre
by a trail of fire. For them nature was still malignant: on
the opening night the customary salutation written by a local
poet (possibly Robinson) was unexpectedly ironic. It was ut-
tered by Mrs. Stark in her customary melodramatic manner; she
began:

> "Could we tonight the eternal slumbers break
> Of Avon's Bard, and bid the dreamer wake,
> The astonished muse would bid the poet turn,
> And sleep again beneath the honored urn...."

As she continued to boom out the verse the audience
gradually became aware that something was wrong with the theatre. Their absorption in Mrs. Stark's passionate verse
could not dispel from their minds the strong feeling that the
theatre was moving -- and they with it. But audiences were
pretty hardy in those days; they remained philosophically in
their seats as the building settled in the rich mud of a
quagmire. Mud was a familiar aspect of the San Francisco scene
and they were not afraid. It was quite common during their
promenades to step casually into mud up to their waists, and
if the building decided to sink into the mud that too could
not be helped. Some of the more meditative ones perhaps spec-
ulated on the possibility that Will Shakespeare's turning in
his grave with unexpected violence had set up vibrations in
the ground that communicated themselves to the now temple of

the Bard. But whatever reactions had been set up in the minds of the audience they did not make for an unalloyed interest in the offering of the evening.

And if it were not some perversity of nature that hampered the cause of drama in San Francisco there were always the unpredictable human factors. It was a small child, an _enfant terrible_, that consummated the Stark disaster at the American and sent them scurrying back into the arms of Tom Maguire.

LITTLE CHARLIE'S BLUNDER

The scene was sometime in December, 1851. a roaring melodrama, _The Stranger_, was being tossed to a lively and appreciative audience. There was love and passion and mother love, all swelling up into a magnificent melodramatic climax: Mrs. Stark moved rapidly across the stage and faced the wings. She fell to her knees and flung out her arms.

"My child!" cried the distraught heroine, and little Charlie Robinson, resplendent in a red plush suit was given a terrific shove onto the stage. Little Charlie was very unhappy: for this, his debut on the stage, he had been awakened out of a very comfortable and satisfying slumber, transported down Telegraph Hill through the fog and mud by his mother, and finally pushed upon the stage. He was sleepy, wet and miserable.

"My child!" repeated Mrs. Stark in a more dramatic and insistent manner. Charlie was blinded by the lights; he

could see nothing but this huge woman in black bearing down upon him, making hideous noises. He did not know whether to be frightened or not.

"MY CHEE-ILD!" she screamed.   Finally Charlie made up his mind; he had forgotten his lines, but he knew what to say and this was also effective.

"↓*(?↓" said Charlie.   This little bit of improvisation brought down the house, sent Mrs. Stark sobbing hysterically off the stage, ended the Starks' season at tne American and sent Dr. Robinson out of the show business.   It also provoked another of the public quarrels in which Mrs. Stark seemed to be constantly involved. She published a letter accusing Mrs. Robinson of having deliberately planned the catastrophe out of jealousy, in order to ruin her.   But Mrs. Robinson had her defenders, and Dr. Robinson closed his theatre with a rousing benefit performance given by the company for Mrs. Robinson, in which little Charlie in the historic red suit was the chief performer.

THE THIRD JENNY LIND

Maguire had built his third most extravagant Jenny Lend in October and now was glad to have the Starks back with him.   They joined the company managed by Junius Brutus Booth Jr., playing from Dec. 8 1851 to January 20, 1852.   The old Shakespearean plays were revived, and even more ambitious ones; the difficult Henry VI was given successfully, with Stark in the role of Falstaff. Although Stark's Falstaff was

amusing enough and proficiently handled it was not one of his best roles; Stark, at home in tragedy, lacked the temperament for comedy. On December 26, however, he achieved the success of the season in his striking interpretation of Iago to Joshua Proctor's Othello.

After their season at the Jenny Lind the Starks gave a few performances at the Adelphi on Dupont Street, playing with Mr. and Mrs. Baker, Frank Chanfrau and Miss Albertine early in March. During April they acquired the lease of the American, and now with no jealous Mrs. Robinson, or precocious little Charlie around to thwart them, they enthusiastically plunged into a new season. This lasted until June 17 at which time the dramatic profession got together at the American and staged a farewell demonstration benefit for James Stark, presenting him with a magnificent gold watch. He left for the East alone. Mrs. Stark continued to play on for the next few months and at the end of September received her benefit.

Stark did not remain very long in New York; he found Forrest, the reigning star, too strongly entrenched to be budged. After a few unsuccessful months he returned to California where his talents were more appreciated. Perhaps his failure was due to the still unfading memory of the Astor Place riots, and to the fact that his style of acting was still patterned after the English actor Macready who had been his master.

17

James Stark was not yet a finished actor; he was an assiduous student, striving constantly to perfect his style. At first his acting was stilted and artificial, like so many of the Shakespearean actors of his day, especially those who were of the Macready school. Even in this pattern the critics found constant and rapid improvement: his face became more expressive, his voice more flexible and nuancé. He was achieving perfection in this particular style, and there were even some who found him better than Forrest.

In December Stark was back in San Francisco. The critical and demonstrative public enthusiastically following his career were anxious to find evidences of improvement. They were not disappointed; the conscientious student had still further improved.

> "Yet," says the critic of the Pioneer, (Jan. 1855) "the tone and action of Macready were about him. He had carried the style to a pitch of perfection, justly entitling him to rank as at least the second American tragedian."

For two full months the Starks played to an admiring audience, presenting the old favorites: The Gamester, Richelieu, Hamlet, and others. Night after night they performed at the American. On March 7, having delayed many times the contemplated visit, they left for Australia, which had begun suddenly to compete with San Francisco as an attraction for actors. There was a gold boom; miners were throwing nuggets on the stage, and there was very little competition for the Starks. They found in Australia a rich harvest. Possibly

because of the British style of their acting they were received with tremendous popularity sweeping all before them
and piling up the nuggets. They extended their visit to fif-
teen months. When they returned to San Francisco on July,
1854 they brought back a fortune of more than $100,000.

But this was not the only result of the Australian
trip. Stark's faithful admirers thronged the Metropolitan on
his return, eager to see what new marvels of technique their
idol had prepared for them. And for the first time they were
disappointed, bitterly disappointed. He had certainly changed -- but it was a change for the worse, they thought: instead of improving he had retrogressed. Was it the climate
of Australia that had affected his acting, or was it financial success? Had riches debased his talents?

ADVERSE CRITICISM

These were the questions they asked considering
themselves shamelessly betrayed by their old favorite. For
the first time the newspapers turned on him. For a week in
August the Starks played at the Metropolitan in the familiar
Richelieu, The Lady of Lyons, Damon and Pythias, Henry IV and
Othello, and the critics attacked them mercilessly after each
performance . The Wide West (Aug. 6, 1854) was especially
severe:

> "Of Richelieu: "Mr. Stark has not improved by
> his visit to Australia, and the mannerisms
> which formerly disfigured his style, are still
> painfully apparent. His rendition of Bulwer's
> splendid creation was by no means what it

should have been. The measured rising and falling of his voice, renders his elocution monot-
onous. Mrs. Stark as Julia de Martemar, did
not add to her previous reputation as an act-
tress."

Of The Lady of Lyons: "On Wednesday evening
the Lady of Lyons was inflicted on an audience
more remarkable for endurance than numbers..."

Of Othello: "Mr. Stark's Othello was marred by
the indistinctness of his utterance in many of
the finest passages--the words blending together as it were, in their passage from his throat.
Booth's Iago would have pleased, but that comparison between him and his father obtruded..."

And yet these had before been considered their best

interpretations. What had happened?

FAVORABLE CRITICISM

At last the perspicacious critic of the Pioneer un-

covered the mystery. It was very simple: the other critics,

he decided were misinterpreting the change. It was not that

Stark had degenerated into the old style; he had changed over

to an altogether new one. Having exhausted the possibilities

of the Macready style, Stark the constant student, had nimbly

deserted it for a fresh one. And naturally he was not so ad-

vanced in the new style as he had been in the old. The

Pioneer, Jan. 1855, welcomes this change, finding in the new

interpretations spontaneity and freshness, comparing him now

to the elder Booth, ranking him now (next to Booth) as the

greatest actor in California:

"From the stilted manner of the olden times,
rendered dear, it is true by the genius of many
of the brightest ornaments of the stage, he has
passed at one leap into the preferable style of

nature....Judging by his Iago and Hamlet he no
longer falls into categories, into a particular
school of acting....He is rising in a peculiar
style of his own....We hail the change, nay,
the reel, although, perhaps to some, not visible
improvement, with gladness....With the exception of the elder Booth his superior has not
been in California....In his faculty for improvement, in his youth, in his love for his
profession, in his unremitting labor, in his
genius, in his conscientiousness--whatever others may say to him--there are high rounds in
his ladder, which he can yet reach...."

In this engagement Stark and another actor called
Neafie were alternating in the principal roles of the tragedies and dramas. The Pioneer considered Neafie as a foil for
the new richness of Stark's acting. According to the critic
it was the antithesis between the physical and the intellectual actor, between the trite stylization, the cold stock man-
nerisms and the "warm and fresh impersonations, coming from
within and appealing to the mind, the heart and the soul."

In concluding this long sympathetic critique the
Pioneer made a few gentle suggestions to Stark, suggestions
for improvement that the student would appreciate. It urged
him to improve his vocal delivery; it found the reading of
Hamlet to be pure and accurate, but reminded him that sometimes the tones of his voice were too faint for the audience
to appreciate the beauties of the language.

On December 25, 1854 the Starks concluded their engagement at the American. They played at Sacramento during
January and February and returned a few months later for a
season at the Metropolitan. On May 6 Stark played at his

wife's benefit and later appeared as Richelieu. During the
month Edwin Booth, who had just returned from Australia,
played Richard III, and the Pioneer of June, 1855 pointing
approvingly at James Stark, chided Booth for devoting too
little time to study.

AUSTRALIA AGAIN

In August the Starks, who had by this time regained
their lost prestige, took over the Union Theatre. They played there until the end of December and then moved their company to the American. Mrs. Stark had her farewell benefit on
February 1, 1856, and on the 4th, Stark received a grand company farewell benefit, for they were leaving the country to
try their luck again in Australia.

But the earlier bonanza could not be repeated. Between 1853 and 1856 there had been many other stars in Sidney
and the novelty of the theatre had perhaps worn off. The
Starks remained in Australia over a year, almost as long as
their previous visit; these were long weary months that dragged before a small apathetic public and finally, with very
little to show for the time, they returned to San Francisco in
May, 1857.

BACK TO SAN FRANCISCO

Their long separation from San Francisco, however,
was this time almost disastrous. The theatrical scene was
constantly changing in San Francisco and it was hard to

re-establish themselves. They succeeded within a few months in securing a short engagement at the American, in August, when Stark played Falstaff in Henry VI and The Merry Wives of Windsor -- and then after a few months idleness and discouragement decided to go back across the plains and see what the East could offer them.

In November, 1857 they left for the East. In his last visit, six years previously, Stark had little success and during this trip his success was only indifferent. In April, 1858 the Starks made their debut at Wallack's Theatre in New York in The Gamester and played a season of their other favorite pieces. In July they returned to San Francisco and in two months were engaged at the Lyceum.

AT THE LYCEUM

From September to November the Starks played at the Lyceum; the supporting company was mediocre and the dramatic fare was inferior: the state of the drama was pretty low at this time in San Francisco. They occasionally revived their old successes: Damon and Pythias, Hamlet, The Gamester, Pizarro, Macbeth, Julius Caesar and introduced The Taming of The Shrew. But with each of these they had to lighten the evening with farces, and they had to produce such paltry material as Clouds and Sunshine; The Apostate, or The Moors of Spain; Napoleon I, or The Fortunes of St. Anlyn; A Struggle of the Heart; The Honeymoon.

23

AT MAGUIRE'S

The next engagement of the Starks was at Maguire's Opera House during the first week of February 1859, playing with Mr. and Mrs. Baker and Junius Booth Jr., beginning with the very popular Hunchback and ending with Stark's personal favorite Othello. In the last piece Stark played Othello; Booth, Iago; Baker, Cassio; Mrs. Baker, Desdemona; and Mrs. Stark, Emilia. In April the Maguire Opera House was reopened, again with The Hunchback and the popular actress Mrs. Judah now a member of the new company. Again some of the old favorites such as Richelieu were given but there were the usual farces and mediocre spectacles, like the tedious military drama, the Veteran and the drama of Therese, or The Orphan of Geneva.

BEGINNING OF DECLINE

On April 29 the Starks returned to the Lyceum, in support of the star, James Anderson. When the Lyceum company transferred to the American for Anderson's farewell engagement Stark assumed the stage management. But Stark was no longer the star and that fact is significant: he was beginning his decline. Illness and fatigue were having their effect; the fire was burning out. Tragedians do not last very long; they are consumed quickly in the flame of passion.

On May 23, 1859 at a benefit to the Hebrew Benevolent Society "the grand old woman," Mrs. Judah, who was to go for thirty years more, was giving another of her famous performances as the Nurse to Mrs. Baker's Juliet, Anderson's

24

Romeo and Stark's Mercutio.

In November and December of 1859 the Starks were back at Maguire's Opera House. Stark had an opportunity to rise to his former level in Macbeth, Richelieu, and Pizarro.

In 1860 the Starks left San Francisco for a tour of the interior, traveling as far as Portland, Oregon. In May 1861 they returned to Maguire's Opera House for a few nights. The tour had been unsatisfactory -- San Francisco on their return was dismally unwelcoming; variety was on the upswing and the legitimate drama was in an anaemic state. Even the Starks could not transfuse any blood into the wreched patient. They started the season ambitiously with a performance of Othello. The Bulletin, May 29, 1861, pleasantly startled, remarked: "It appears that we are now to have a round of the legitimate" and announced that Julius Caesar and King John were in rehearsal. But they never got around to them. On June 8, 1861 The Bulletin reports a benefit for Stark. Typical of the state of the drama in those days was the programme which announced incongruously:

> "A portion of the second act of Henry VI, including the death scene; the farce of Jumbo Jim."

> "The drama of the Irish Emigrant, or Temptation vs Riches."

> "The beneficiary," concludes the programme, "will appear as King Henry in the first piece and O'Brien in the last."

READINGS FROM THE POETS

Drama was being submerged under the flood of

variety and minstrelsy and those actors who were able to do so were deserting the sinking ship. In those days it was very useful to be a competent tight-rope walker or juggler as well as a tragedian. But Mr. Stark could neither sing or dance nor crack jokes; he was a tragedian. He was also not a very good carpenter but they didn't need any incompetent carpenters in San Francisco just then. So Mr. Stark without a stage and a company to play with did the next best thing; he became the whole play himself.

PUBLIC INDIFFERENCE

On June 13, 1861 Stark began a series of readings from the poets and dramatists at Tucker's Academy of Music. He had during his acting career studiously cultivated his voice and was an admirable elocutionist. Whatever illusions Mr. Stark had about the poets and dramatists, however, were quickly shattered: variety had set a new fashion in the theatre and the public wanted lively entertainment. So for his second series of readings, on June 17 -- the anniversary of the Battle of Bunker Hill -- he recited a new national ode, "written by a gentleman of this city"; also, The Battle of Bunker Hill and O'Flannigan and the Fairies. During this evening of "choice readings from the poets and dramatists" a band played occasional pieces. The Bulletin of June 22, 1861 said seriously:

> "Without the sensation and nervous excitement
> of theatrical performance, the present style of

entertainment will naturally please and abundantly satisfy the many persons who never dream of entering a play house, and who yet have poetic feeling, taste and imagination to be gratified."

But what Mr. Stark was really doing was producing his own form of vaudeville, reduced to the taste of vaudeville patrons.

Again on June 27 he delivered some patriotic recitations at a grand national concert at Platts Hall: the occasion was an impressive one, many national notables were present. Mr. Stark did his part for his country and probably acquitted himself nobly, but he was not in his element: he would have been much more at home in Shakespeare.

OPENING OF THE METROPOLITAN

Just when Stark was about to consider the plight of the drama as hopeless and was about to abandon San Francisco in his despair, John Torrence opened the new Metropolitan Theatre. A new company had been formed consisting of all the available dramatic talent in the city: Mrs. Judah, Miss Mowbray, John Wood, H. Courtaine, Frank Mayo, D. C. Anderson, and others -- and James Stark was called to head the company as star. On July 1, Stark opened at the Metropolitan; temporarily the decline was arrested.

The opening of the new theatre was a spectacular one. An immense enthusiastic audience crowded the house. They received the opening salutation written by Mrs. Hossmer

with interest; they received with cheers the patriotic passage declaimed by the practiced Mr. Stark:

> "We see again Columbia's honored land,
> Wrenched by our fathers from the oppressor's hand.
> And all inspired by what has passed away,
> Feel that self-same spirit glows today
> And the land their sacred blood set free
> Shall be a Union until Eternity!
> Untorn, our Stars and Stripes shall float on high
> Long as their kindred orbs illume the sky!"

With their spirit exalted by this patriotic lyricism it was to be expected, that the feeble comedy, The Love
Chase which followed, rather dragged...."

Stark remained at the Metropolitan for the next few
months, but it was obvious that he was not happy there.   He
was compelled to act in a series of tawdry dramas and farces,
he, James Stark, who had once been the Melancholy Dane, and
the Jealous Moor.   Frustration, the strain of acting, illness financial difficulties, were contributing to his down-
fall. And like the traditional actor that he was,he succumbed easily to liquor. But he was the foremost elocutionist in
San Francisco and at a benefit for the cause of Temperance
held at Platts Hall on July 23 he was called upon to declaim
a tribute to the American Flag, which he did in a stirring
and patriotic manner despite a slight intoxication.

STARK RETIRES FOR THREE YEARS

In November James Stark gave his last performance
at the Metropolitan and then suddenly disappeared from San
Francisco.   For three years he retired from the stage while

28

Mrs. Stark carried on for him, performing at the Metropolitan and the Eureka. She was very active during these years and on December 25, 1863 she took over the lease of the Metropolitan with Mrs. Emily Jordan and ran it until March, 1864. She had been all her life too closely associated with the stage (through marriage and otherwise) not to maintain some connection with the theatre.

ATTEMPTS COMEBACK

She greeted her husband when he returned in January 1864 after three years absence to play at her theatre. But Stark had by now lost much of the popularity he once had with the San Francisco public. On January 27 he made his reappearance at Mrs. Stark's benefit, playing in his favorite role, as Cardinal Richelieu, and as Petruchio in The Taming of the Shrew; his wife played opposite him as Julia de Mortimer and Katherine. However the public was apathetic and on February 2 he played his farewell benefit. The next day he left for the East.

Two months later Stark was back, but a nervous restlessness seems to have possessed him. He stayed for only a little while in San Francisco and then was off again. During the next few years we hear of occasional appearances in the interior, at Salt Lake City, Portland. Bad luck seemed constantly to be pursuing him; at one time a wealthy man his fortune had been almost entirely dissipated by unwise speculation. Again like the traditional actor he was generous

and improvident and with absolutely no practical business sense. In February, 1868 he returned to California to find still another misfortune confronting him: by a reversal of a decision of the Supreme Court he lost the title to a large and valuable property. And then came the final blow -- his wife divorced him. Now without her good sense and firm support he tumbled recklessly to disaster.

TRIES AUSTRALIA AGAIN

He tried desperately to forestall the inevitable by a return trip to Australia. He remembered the first trip there in 1853 with Mrs. Stark when they had amassed a fortune; perhaps there was still another chance. In June 1868 we hear of him running a theatre in Melbourne; but this venture did not prosper, and in January, 1869 he was back in San Francisco. His health and morale shattered he hunted around wildly for still another possible public; then he hit upon it -- the mining camps. Other actors who had failed elsewhere had been able to exploit the liberality of the miners; his mind turned back to his first glorious season in San Francisco in 1850 at the old Jenny Lind, where he had played Shakespeare for the miners and they had loved it. There was still a chance: he would return to the miners and he would return to Shakespeare.

STRICKEN BY PARALYSIS

On February 25, 1869 he left for Carson City and a

tour of the mines. On May 11 the end came: while playing at Virginia City, Nevada he was stricken with paralysis--never to recover. This was the end of James Stark, the tragedian. His actual death was dragged out over a period of six years. But the acting profession remembering his former greatness and generosity would not let him starve. They staged benefits for him; gave him small parts to play. But the end for this ruin of a great actor could not much longer be delayed.

DEATH OF JAMES STARK

On October 12, 1875 the celebrated Edwin Booth was exciting applause in New York playing Hamlet. Playing a very negligible role in the tragedy was an obscure actor named James Stark: James Stark was now forgotten but at one time, twenty five years ago, when Booth had been a boy in San Francisco struggling for recognition, James Stark had been hailed as one of the greatest interpreters not only of Hamlet but also of Othello, Richelieu, Macbeth, Richard III and King Lear. Possibly James Stark now reflected on the transience of human glory, possibly he made some tragic gesture -- and when the curtain fell on Shakespeare's tragedy, his own tragedy came to a bitter end. James Stark made his exit from the stage of life. . . .

MRS. STARK REMARRIES

But the career of the indefatigable Mrs. Stark was still flourishing. After her divorce from her third husband,

31

James Stark, she married a Dr. Gray of New York.   She was no longer taking any more chances with unstable and impermanent actors;   this Dr. Gray had no connection **with** the   stage and had a very large fortune.   But even this did not help; and after his death she returned with resignation to her destiny.

MRS. STARK'S FIFTH MARRIAGE

Her fifth husband was Charles R. Thorne, the veteran actor and manager.   Mrs. Sarah Kirby Wingered Stark Gray Thorne now became the stepmother of two important actors of San Francisco, Charles R. Thorne Jr., for many years leading man at Maguire's Opera House, and Edwin Thorne, star for many seasons of The Black Flag. By the time of Thorne's death she must have been taking on the proportions of a legend.   In 1897 she was reported as still in San Francisco, still defying decay, in her own peculiar way becoming a substantial institution in San Francisco, a whole theatrical tradition in herself, a symbol of the city which survives catastrophe after catastrophe and yet continues its confident indomitable course. . . .

CRITICAL ESTIMATE OF STARK

And as for James Stark, who was but one incident in her very eventful life -- where does he fit into the variegated pattern of the San Francisco theatre?   He was perhaps not one of the very great American actors; for he was not born on the stage.   He tried very hard, but he lived a dissolute life.   Even the most persevering study cannot compen-

sate for lack of genius. Thus an article in the _Overland Monthly_ of July 1923 reviewing the careers of the Hamlets of San Francisco says of James Stark:

> "His Hamlet was a very clever exhibition of mimetic art, but it lacked the soul, the effective realism given to it later by both Edwin Booth and Edwin L. Davenport."

But even if James Stark was not a great actor his effect on the tradition of the San Francisco stage was not a trivial one. In the crude and coarse San Francisco of 1850 he helped to introduce a taste for good acting, for fine drama, for exalted tragedy. As much as any other single individual he contributed generously to the brilliance of the early theatre of San Francisco.

33

JAMES STARK

Representative Parts Taken By Stark.

Date	Role	Play
1850	Damon	Damon and Pythias
	Othello	Othello
	Virginius	Virginius
	Hamlet	Hamlet
	Cardinal Richelieu	Richelieu
	Norval	Douglas
	Rollo	Pizarro
	Jaffe	Venice Preserved
	Iago	Othello
	Macbeth	Macbeth
	Shylock	The Merchant of Venice
	King Lear	King Lear
	Petrucchio	Taming of the Shrew
	Ruy Gomez	Ruy Gomez
	Dazzle	London Assurance
	The Stranger	The Stranger
1852	Falstaff	Henry IV
1853	Richard III	Richard III
	Beverly	The Gamester
1854	Master Walter	The Hunchback
	Brutus	Julius Caesar
	Coriolanus	Coriolanus
	Alfred Evelyn	Money
1857	Falstaff	Merry Wives of Windsor
1858	Brutus	Julius Caesar

34

THE STARKS

BIBLIOGRAPHY

Leman, Walter M.   Memories of an Old Actor.   (San Francisco,
     A. Roman Company, 1886; p. 247)

McCabe, James H. Journal (Mss.   bound,   Sutro Library, (San
     Francisco)

Rourke, Constance   Troupers of the Gold Coast or The Rise   of
     Lotta Crabtree.   (New York. Harcourt,   Brace   and   Company
     1928; pp. 33-37)

NEWSPAPERS AND PERIODICALS

Evening Picayune (San Francisco) Feb. 23, 28, 28, Nov.4,12-18,
     26-29, Dec. 2-5, 12-16, 1850; Jan. 28, Feb. 5-8, 1851.

Alta California   (San Francisco)   Dec. 19, 21,   23,   25, 29,
     1850; Feb. 29, March 7, 11, 14, 15, 1851.

Golden Era (San Francisco) Jan. 2, 3, Feb. 20,   March 6, 1853;
     August 13, 1854.

Wide West   (San Francisco) April 23,   Aug. 6, 1854; June 7,
     Aug. 23, 30, Sept. 13, Nov. 1857.

The Pioneer   (San Francisco)   Jan., April, May, June 1855.

Daily Evening Bulletin (San Francisco) Nov. 2, 1857; Oct. 6-
     9,11-22, 29, Nov. 1, 13, 15, 20, 1858; Jan. 13, Feb. 1,   8,
     April 6, 20, 26, 29, May 7, 9, 23, Nov. 17, 19, 28, Dec. 2,
     12, 13, 1859; Nov. 2-11, 1860; May 29, June 8, 10, 13,   17,
     20, 22, 27, July 1, 2, 23, 27, Sept. 13, Nov. 13, 1861; Jan.
     27, Feb. 1, 2, 1864; May, Sept. 1869; March 13, 1897.

The Spirit of the Times   (New York) Feb. 5, 8, 29, June 12,
     1868; May 12, 19, Sept. 13, 14, 1869.

Overland Monthly   (San Francisco) July 1923.

TABLE OF CONTENTS

THE BAKERS

(John Lewis Baker, 1825-1873) (Mrs Baker, 1822-1887)

JOHN LEWIS BAKER

(1825 - 1873)

PHOTO FROM ODELL'S ANNALS OF THE NEW YORK STAGE

ALEXINA FISHER BAKER

(1822 - 1887)

35

THE BAKERS

Pioneer Actor-Managers

The very first season of the San Francisco theatre
was interrupted by a somewhat inefficient manager. That gentleman calmly gambled away the proceeds of the first week, and
thus the season abruptly came to an end.

This incident created a bad precedent for the San
Francisco theatre. For some time after that its career was
marvelously punctuated by all sorts of accidents, hilarious
and catastrophic. The audiences welcomed, in addition to
the scheduled performance, the unexpected treat. They were
not sure whether the walls would burn down around them, the
floor sink beneath them, whether the leading lady would shoot
the first walking gentleman, or whether everybody would forget their lines altogether. But they knew that something
would happen and some of the things that did happen have by
now become legendary.

The audiences were enthusiastic and they welcomed
these diversions. The actors likewise were enthusiastic and
they were anxious to please and to make money. Various companies arrived in San Francisco; competition arrived. A wild

race set in. Everything was impermanent, unsettled, agitated.
The important thing was to make money quickly.

CHAOTIC THEATRICAL TIMES

Enthusiasm led to excess.   Colors became gaudier,
noises louder.   The public had to be stimulated, amused, exalted. Companies offered quantity and diversity: a different
performance every night, special novelties, featured attractions.   Night after night they hurled their tragedies, spectacles, farces at their audiences; and the tragedies became
heavier; the spectacles, more spectacular; the farces,   more
farcical.   Night after night the dramas became more grandiose, more esoteric, more dizzy.   And the audiences were pro-
portionately awed and dazzled.

Such trivial details as learning their lines prop-
erly or remaining semi-sober while on the stage did not over-
ly concern the actors.   As they bombarded the suffering audiences with their uneven rhetoric they considered that the
pretentiousness of their offerings and the exuberance of their
acting would atone for minor faults.

If there was rivalry between troupes there was
greater rivalry within each company.   Professional and personal jealousies constantly flared up into violent outbreaks;
casts were broken up daily; shootings, suicides cut ugly gaps
in the seasons.   The most brilliant actors were the most un-
dependable.   Such excellent performers as the Starks, for
example, were very flighty -- constantly involved in violent

quarrels and scandalous scrapes.

By the middle of 1853 the San Francisco theatre seemed to be in a hopelessly confused state. This undisciplined exuberance began to pall on the audiences; they demanded more solid substance, more adequate preparation. Audiences were already becoming hyper-critical. They were getting a little tired of Shakespeare, especially a Shakespeare excruciatingly performed. In fact Shakespeare by this time was falling into disrepute in San Francisco. Said the _Alta California_ of November 28:

> "Circumstances will hardly justify the introduction of Shakespeare's tragedies on the California stage. To those who do not understand the usual merits of the play, it is a dull and uninteresting spectacle; while those who can appreciate its beauty, lose its effect in the manner in which it is delineated."

Inefficient and tactless managers, undisciplined and incompetent actors, shoddy plays and mutilated texts, lack of suitable equipment -- all these elements were conspiring to drive the public away from the theatre altogether.

BAKERS INTRODUCE A REFORMATION

Into this muddled picture stepped the Bakers, John Lewis and his wife, Alexina Fisher. On March 2, 1853 the Bakers announced the opening, under their management, of the little French theatre on Dupont Street called the Adelphi. They had arrived in San Francisco a year previously and had already acquired considerable reputation as actors. Alexina Fisher Baker had already conquered the affections of the

public by her charm and lady-like qualities; John Lewis
Baker was esteemed as a strong minor performer, an actor of
the romantic school in spite of an unimpressive appearance. He
was very short and had a "remarkably prominent, ulta-aquiline
nose." But now he had an opportunity to demonstrate his fine
ability as a manager.

There was abundant talent in San Francisco at this
time; what was needed was organizational ability, discipline.
It was no small task to bring order out of the chaotic confu-
sion of the theatre in San Francisco; but Lewis Baker succeeded in steering it out of the wretched by-paths onto a
broad triumphant highway. He started the glorious new tradition and thus his importance to the San Francisco theatre
is inestimable.

There were other managers in San Francisco before
Lewis Baker: Charles R. Thorne, James Stark and James Evrard;
but Baker surpassed them all. He introduced the idea of discipline, the necessary basis for all aritstic enterprises.
He created a new level for the San Francisco theatre, and
what is most important, he brought audiences back to the theatre. "If Mrs. Baker inaugurated a new era for the California stage" (says Catherine Coffin Phillips in Portsmouth
Plaza) "Lewis Baker set a new standard in management. He was
the dean of San Francisco theatre managers."

Lewis Baker had considerable preparation for his
career as actor-manager on the San Francisco stage. Although
still a young man -- only 27 -- when he arrived with his

newly-married wife in February 1852 to play a brief engagement at the Jenny Lind, he had successfully been an actor and manager in various theatres of the east and the west. He was born in Philadelphia in 1825 -- but during his boyhood his family moved to Texas. Texas was virgin territory and here he had his first opportunity to gratify his interest in the theatre. He made his debut, significantly enough, as a manager; he founded a new theatre in the city of Galveston. When the Mexican War broke out in 1848 he was at Corpus Christi where General Taylor's division was stationed, abundantly performing his patriotic duty: running two theatres simultaneously. The war over he traveled back to the east, played in New York, Boston and Philadelphia. In the latter city he met the lovely Alexina Fisher, then Philadelphia's reigning favorite, and married her in May 1851. A few months later they set sail for the El Dorado.

In San Francisco they found immediate favor. A week after their arrival -- on February 14, 1852 -- they made their debut at Maguire's Jenny Lind Theatre -- the third and most permanent of that name. They played in The Hunchback, even at that early date an old favorite in San Francisco and through the years to come destined to be played ad nauseam. Their "Master Walter" and "Julia" at once aroused enthusiasm, no small feat considering that the very popular and capable Starks had previously starred in these roles in the same theatre. For twenty-one nights they played to crowded houses. This was both a record and a precedent. They demonstrated

that it was not necessary to change the bill every night if
you had a good play and good actors and good management. And
the moribund theatre of San Francisco was being quickened into life. San Francisco's passionate interest in the drama
was being revived. Soon after the Bakers' arrival three theatres were running simultaneously.

But this successful first season of the Bakers did
not entirely solve the theatrical problem of the day. It was
almost entirely a personal triumph for Mrs. Baker. According
to the Annals of San Francisco Mrs. Baker was "the chief and
only attraction, the company generally being poor, and insuf-
ficiently conducted." In short, a good manager was still
needed: Lewis Baker had not yet stepped in to assume his
rightful role.

MRS. BAKER TRIUMPHS

Alexina Fisher Baker created an immediate impression. The newspapers were full of admiring comments. From
the Alta California after her first performance (Feb.15,1852).

> "There is a freshness and simplicity and at the
> same time a finish in the acting of Mrs. Baker
> that will make her as popular as they have
> elsewhere."

At their benefit on February 20 when she played
Juliet in Romeo and Juliet there was an echo of her former
triumphs. At the close of her performance she was called before the curtain to be showered with bouquets. To one of
these was attached a diamond ring, a ring described by the
Alta as being "of most exquisite workmanship, containing nine

stones, and valued at $350." And on the inside was engraved:
"Auld lang syne." It was the gift of an expatriate Phila-
delphian who had admired Alexina Fisher in Philadelphia and
was overjoyed at renewing an "auld acquaintance."

Alexina Fisher Baker possessed that certain personal charm and magnetism which immediately captivate audiences
and transcend mere acting ability. In Lights and Shades in
San Francisco she is called "the most adored of the theatre-
going public." She was among the first of the San Francisco
stream of favorite actresses, for this was a time when women
dominated the theatrical scene, not only as actresses but as
managers. In this almost completely man's town it was the
women who ruled in the gaming-houses and the theatre; ruled
by virtue of glamor and fascination and sentiment. Those
rough miners had the traditional susceptible hearts and they
succumbed readily and regularly to those charming and lovely
and gifted ladies who paraded in and out of the San Francisco
theatrical scene such as Mrs. Baker, Caroline Chapman, Mrs.
Judah, Matilda Heron, Laura Keene, Catherine Sinclair, Madame
Biscaccianti, Kate Hayes, Anna Bishop, Lola Montez, Ada Isaacs
Menken,

But in the case of Mrs. Baker it was not only the
woman who was admired but the accomplished actress. Whereas
the interest of Lewis Baker in the theatre was an acquired
one, Mrs. Baker's attachment was hereditary: she was born on
the stage -- an evident requirement for those who aspire to
be great actors -- a member of the fairly well-known Fisher

family. In fact, one of her sisters, Oceana Fisher, had
joined her on her expedition to San Francisco and later became a member of the famous Adelphi company.

Alexina Fisher was born in Frankfort, Kentucky, in
1822 and made her debut in New York. After several seasons
in New York she went to Philadelphia: she was at once adopt-
ed into the hearts of the Philadelphians. In San Francisco
where every exaggeration was carried to excess Mrs. Baker was
even more violently adored. Perhaps the refinement of her
manners exercised some influence. With the usual array of
superlatives which constituted the journalistic jargon of the
day the Golden Era (Dec. 19, 1852) explains:

> "...there is no better actress, or more worthy
> lady in this country ...Mrs. Baker was for
> several years the acknowledged favorite in
> Philadelphia, and no actress of the day was
> more honored for her ladylike attributes in
> public and private life. In California she
> has acquired a reputation no less enviable."

In contrast to their rough lives and crude manners
the miners could appreciate gentle gestures and ladylike ways.
And because their world was coarse and harsh they could enter
a theatre and be moved by poetry.

Her contemporaries found in Alexina Baker a gift for
poetic interpretation. Murdoch described her as "... by nature ardent and impulsive... As an actress she embodied the
poetical ideal of the characters she personated." Mrs. Baker
was now the shining star on the San Francisco horizon.

But Lewis Baker, whose small acting talents had been

eclipsed during the Jenny Lind season by the brilliance of his wife, was quietly planning for himself an independent career. When the Adelphi fell idle for a short time he used this as his opportunity to make his managerial debut in San Francisco. With his wife he engaged the services of the Starks, Frank Chanfrau, and Miss Albertine in forming the new company. Each one of these was a star and had already established a reputation: the Starks as pioneer tragedians; Chanfrau (who was Baker's brother-in-law) for his solid acting in his specialized role of a tough city boy; Albertine as an accomplished dancer.

FIRST VENTURE A FAILURE

On March 2, 1852 this "most powerful combination of talent ever presented to the San Francisco public" according to the Golden Era, opened at the Adelphi. This was the first and last night of the season. Baker was defeated in his first venture as a manager.

The cause of this disaster was the usual one that blighted the growth of the San Francisco theatre at this time: lack of discipline, the flightiness of actors. Miss Coad, one of the members of the company, suddenly took it into her head to join Booth's troupe, and the very temperamental Starks, their esthetic feelings injured by a casual remark made by another member, had withdrawn in a huff on the opening night. The Bakers had no opportunity to brood over this initial defeat, for a few days later they began a two-weeks engage-

ment at the American, and from there they left on a trip to
Sacramento.

On April 12,1852 they were back in San Francisco to
play another engagement at the Jenny Lind for two months, and
then they left on a tour of the mining towns. On August 21
with Mr. Thoman and Mrs. Judah they reopened the Adelphi, and
a new era in the history of the San Francisco theatre began.

BAKER SCORES WITH THE ADELPHI

The failure of the first managerial venture at the
Adelphi had taught the Bakers the necessity of tact and discipline in dealing with temperamental actors and during the
months that followed as they played in San Francisco, Sacramento, Nevada, Grass Valley and Placerville, they had ample
opportunity to study audiences and their tastes: they found
that audiences were becoming very critical about acting and
settings; that they were getting sated with heavy tragedy and
blood and thunder drama;they wanted their plays more finished-
closer to life.

Lewis Baker had observed this refinement of the public taste and during the six months that followed the first
trial at the Adelphi he was carefully preparing a program. On
August 21, 1852 the Adelphi opened with Fazio, a melodrama in
the public taste. The presence of Mrs. Judah,already achieving a reputation as "the grand old woman of the western stage"
and Thoman, a popular interpreter of light comedy roles, as
supporting actors, helped to insure their success. Gradually

the Bakers built up a strong supporting company, composed of
actors who could be disciplined, who could subordinate petty
jealousies and animosities to the welfare of the troupe. Because Lewis Baker was a tactful and industrious leader he
could keep the company intact at the Adelphi as they played
night after night for the incredible season of nine months and
could take the same company to the American where they played
for another long period. The company formed a loyal family
presided over genially and firmly by their juvenile patriarch;
they were a phenomenon in San Francisco; the first really sta-
ble company to play there.

While the contemporary of the Adolphi, the competing
American was a victim of all the faults that had up to this
time characterized the theatre of San Francisco -- changing
management rapidly from Joseph Proctor to D.C. Anderson, to
Mrs. Stark, to a joint stock company, to Proctor again; playing season after season of dull, repetitious stock pieces --
Baker inaugurated a new policy which was enthusiastically ac-
claimed: he introduced an entirely new trend in the San
Francisco theatre toward humbler drama. The public was sur-
feited with the exotic, the rhetorical, and the spectacular;
they were clamoring for the more familiar, the more homely.
And the Bakers gave it to them; they gave them Dickens --
Dickens beautifully dramatized. While at the same time audiences at the American were groaning through Macbeth, they gave
them carefully finished productions, plays taken from familiar
stories and histories. Bringing down the level of the drama

in one respect, they raised it in another. The Bakers were a stabilizing influence. That is their importance in the San Francisco theatre.

ACHIEVING FAME AS A MANAGER

Lewis Baker was a conscientious and industrious manager; he insisted meticulously on details, on abundant rehearsals. Settings and costumes were accurate and complete. He spared no expense to insure the artistic success of their productions;nevertheless on May 9, 1853 when the Adelphi season closed, after playing nine months every day except Sundays, there was an estimated profit of $30,000. Phillips,in Portsmouth Plaza calculates:

> "With the rent of $30,000 a year, a salary of
> $3,000 a week, and musicians, painters and car-
> penters paid the high prevailing wages, and
> with two other theatres carrying superior casts,
> the distinguished success of the Bakers is proof
> of their superiority in their respective ca-
> pacities as manager and leading lady."

These expenses do not include the frequently high salaries paid to stars which often exceed $6,000 for six successive performances; nor the additional expenses for such incidentals as lighting, printing, advertising, costumes, supernumeraries, etc. And when one considers that the Adelphi was a tiny theatre, scarcely seating a few hundred, the courage of the Bakers in making this venture seems much like rashness.

Yet though he insisted on artistic finish and was assiduous about details, Baker was scarcely an idealist; he

was, in fact, shrewd and perspicacious.   He had merely real-
ized a fact to which the other managers were blind; namely,
that the San Francisco public was growing up, and that if the
theatre expected to survive in San Francisco it could not remain crude and puerile.   His judgment was backed by crowded
houses every night, the praise of the critics,the distinction
that he had done more than any other single individual to influence the course of the drama in San Francisco. He had
created the first "temple of legitimate drama" in San Francisco. The critics could now boast that their city possessed
a theatre "fully equal to...the best...in New York and Philadelphia."   (Annals of San Francisco)

     Fazio of the first night was followed by other semi-
popular melodramas like The Duke's Wager and Agnes de Vere,
the audiences liked it.   There were many performances of the
ever-popular Hunchback with Mrs. Baker playing "Julia", the
role that had made her instantly popular at her debut in San
Francisco.   It was at one of these performances,the occasion
of Mrs. Baker's benefit December 19, 1852 that her sister,
Oceana Fisher, made her California debut as "Helen". The
addition of Miss Fisher completed a very proficient company,
consisting of the original founders: the Bakers,Mrs.Judah
and J. Thoman; and Miss E. Coad, Miss Montague, H. F. Daly,
J. H. Vinson, H. H. Coad, J. B. Walton, L. F. Rand, Milne,
Morton, Beatty, Dumfries and others.

     The year 1853 found the troupe at the Adelphi still

going strong. On January 16, 1853 they had been playing over
130 nights and neither the public nor the critics showed signs
of being tired of them.   On this date the "sterling comedy"
Wild Oats was being performed at the Adelphi;at the same time
the Starks,with J. Proctor and D. C. Anderson were playing in
Venice Preserved at the American;at the San Francisco Theatre
Dr. Robinson,the Junius Brutus Booths and the George Chapmans
were in All is not Gold that Glitters.   These were three excellent companies playing in three excellent plays, and   audiences were flocking to all three theatres. The new princi-
ple established by the Bakers had triumphed;new life had been
infused into the San Francisco theatre;audiences had returned
to acclaim the change.

          The critics now began to take a new pride in the San
Francisco theatre and were becoming sensitive to any insult.
The Golden Era,of January 16, 1853 in giving the casts of the
above plays thus prefixed the notice:

> "A San Francisco correspondent of one of the
> Boston papers, in speaking of theatricals in
> California, said in a recent letter that the
> performances at our theatres were not worth pa-
> tronizing, and that our best actors were hardly
> fourth rate.   Our intention is to reply that
> its author is a poor critic or else has thus
> sought to disparage our players through revenge
> for being struck from the 'deadheads.'   In
> order that Boston friends may see we are not
> behind the age we will give the casts of sev-
> eral pieces produced at our theatres during
> the past week."

          The Bakers seemed during this period to be stressing
comedy.   Besides Wild Oats, which the Golden Era of January
9, 1853 found to be "the most entertaining and pleasing   yet

produced" they were presenting such well known comedies as
Sheridan's racy _Critic_. There was a noticeable dearth of
bombastic tragedy; those produced were of a more substantial
nature.

On March 13, 1853 Mrs. Baker played for the first
time the part of young Norval in the tragedy of _Douglas_. And
next week when she played the title role of _Evadne_ the same
critic of the _Golden Era_ (March 20, 1853) raved:

> "The tragedy of Evadne, as produced at the Adel-
> phi last evening, was the most perfect perform-
> ance, in all its departments, we have ever wit-
> nessed in this country. Mrs. Baker as Evadne, a
> character requiring the most careful and labored
> discrimination, proved herself, in our opinion,
> to be without a rival on the American Stage."

In summing up the season the same _Golden Era_ (March
6, 1853) remarked:

> "In the production of legitimate plays and stand-
> ard pieces, the management have been eminently
> successful, and have raised the drama to a point
> never before reached in California, and in the
> crowded and intelligent audiences which nightly
> witness their performances, they have the most
> crowning proof that their exertions are fully
> appreciated."

On May 7, 1853 the triumphant season of the Bakers
at the Adelphi came to an end. They had left their mark on
the San Francisco scene; they had created a new tradition for
the San Francisco theatre; their work was achieved. But having elevated the standard of the drama they were reluctant to
let it drop to a less exalted rank. So they remained longer
in San Francisco. Five days after the close of the Adelphi
season they transferred their company to the American.

50

MANAGER OF THE AMERICAN

The American had been renovated for the occasion; it had been "tastefully arranged," and was now "the most magnificent and elegant theatre in California." (Golden Era March 10, 1853)   The play selected for the opening on March 12, 1853 was Bulwer's The Lady of Lyons, a play which Mrs. Kirby had introduced to San Francisco at her debut two years before, but which had since become Mrs. Baker's favorite vehicle.   During their career in San Francisco the prestige of the Bakers had not only disciplined the temperamental actors; it had also been operating on the audiences, subduing their rowdyish tendencies.   In commenting on the audience of the American first night the Golden Era of May 15, 1853 described it as:

> "...the largest and most refined audience that has ever assembled within the walls of a theatre in this State."

Further on the comments take on a more realistic turn as the critic describes some new managerial equipment:

> "It is due to the managers to state that an efficient police force has been engaged, who will use their utmost authority in preserving order."

The brilliant and prosperous Adelphi season was almost equalled at the American.   Under the management of the Bakers beginning in May, 1853 it became the most important theatre in San Francisco; its ascendancy was finally ended with the opening of the even more elegant Metropolitan by Mrs. Sinclair on December 24, 1853.

51

In July 1853 Catherine Sinclair came to **San** Francisco carrying about her an air of attractive notoriety. She was immediately hired by the Bakers and exhibited at the American. As a "special novelty attraction" Mrs. Baker and Mrs. Sinclair played on consecutive nights the role of Lady Gay Spanker in London Assurance. In case the audience and critics did not entirely grasp the idea the "novelty attraction" was made even more special. On July 24 they alternated as Lady Spanker in different acts of the play!

Even the "special novelty attractions," however, could not overcome the fickleness of the public. During the summer the enthusiasm stirred up by the Bakers had begun to abate in intensity. The audiences needed a breathing spell and during the fall attendance declined. The newspapers claimed that the high prices charged by the theatres were responsible for the thinning audiences; the managers blamed the prices on greater expenses. In the Alta California of August 26, 1853 Baker offered an explanation of the involved finances of the American; he claimed that the regular nightly expenses of the theatre were $600, and during Murdoch's engagement were increased to $1000.

With the engagements of Mrs. Sinclair and Murdoch the Bakers had inaugurated a new policy, augmenting the regular Adelphi company with eastern stars. But now as a general depression hit the San Francisco theatre the triumphant career of Baker as manager was temporarily halted. Increased expenses for stars were not being compensated by increased

attendance. C. R. Thorne, who followed Murdoch in October, played for a while for the Bakers and then, disgruntled by the meager audience, packed up and left.

In December 1853, however, the theatres began to pick up: the Bakers regained their popularity and featuring Caroline Chapman, an early San Francisco favorite,were again attracting crowds with a production of <u>Faustus</u>.   On December 24 Mrs. Sinclair and Murdoch opened the New Metropolitan; and now,the tide having definitely turned in the right direction, people were rushing back to the theatres.

On January 1, 1854 the <u>Golden Era</u>, taking annual stock of the theatrical situation, observed that two theatres were open every night; these were the Metropolitan, where Murdoch, Mrs. Sinclair and their company were playing,   and American:

> "...the American, the scene of a thousand tri-
> umphs -- (where our brilliant Stark was wont to
> move as a 'star' of dazzling effulgence) -- we
> find Mrs. Baker, the incomparable artiste, the
> gem of the social circle -- and here, too, tow-
> ering 'a head and shoulder above them all,'
> can be seen the sparkling eyes and benevolent
> face of Mrs. Judah,who is ever greeted by plau-
> dits of admiring thousands."

TEMPORARILY DESERT SAN FRANCISCO

The new year began splendidly,but then suddenly the theatre had another slump.   The spring season was less pros-· perous, even for the Bakers.   After an unprecedented run of thin houses they closed the American and fled to Sacramento. But in February they were back, to present the Proctors   to

53

San Francisco. On March 5, 1854 the Proctors departed for the East. Soon after the Bakers followed them.

The Bakers had an astonishing success in San Francisco. Their ability as actors, their acumen as managers had gleaned them, it was rumored, as much as a million dollars. And in return they had bequeathed to San Francisco a permanent theatre.

RETURN TO SAN FRANCISCO -- AT THE OPERA HOUSE

In November, 1858 the Bakers returned to San Francisco. Although they had been away from this city almost five years their loyal admirers had not forgotten them. Two weeks after their arrival they began an engagement at Maguire's Opera House. They received a tremendous welcome as they made their first appearance in a new Boucicault play, Pauvrette; the crowded house frequently interrupted the play to roar their applause; the Bakers were repeatedly called before the curtain after each act. At the end of the play Mrs. Baker took her curtain call alone; then suddenly as if at a concerted signal the stage was showered with dozens of beautiful bouquets. In the front of the house, beaming, were the washed faces and pressed suits of the gentlemen of the Pennsylvania Fire Engine Company. Philadelphia had not forgotten.

Mr. Baker made his little speech before the curtain acknowledging the tribute for his wife and himself; very fervently he expressed their appreciation of the various qualities of San Francisco, saying that they expected to remain

permanently in San Francisco and to make this city their home.
He spoke very convincingly and the audience redoubled   their
applause.

This, the Bakers' second and last visit to San Francisco, was to last only a year and a half; but possibly Baker
was sincere in his promise.   Perhaps he was carried away by
the exuberance of the welcome, and on their appearance   things
did look very promising for the drama. A week later   Lewis
Baker took over his new duties as stage manager for Maguire's
Opera House.

Variety was on the upward swing in San Francisco but
had not as yet made great depredations on the popularity   of
the legitimate drama.   There   were still several good   actors
left in San Francisco to struggle against the   dominance   of
variety: with the Bakers at the Opera House were   the dependable and everlasting Mrs. Judah, Mr. Courtaine, Mr. Stevens
and Miss Grattan; in a few months they were joined by the
Starks.   At the Lyceum were J. B. Booth, Woodward and the
Gougenheim sisters.

MRS. BAKER QUELLS A RIVAL

The Gougenheim girls, considering their popularity
menaced by the advent of Mrs.Baker, conceived a master-stroke:
they would take the fight out into the open; they would challenge Mrs. Baker to a duel.

On December 1 the newspapers announced the simul-
taneous productions at the Lyceum and   the   Opera House of

Pauvrette,with Adelaide Gougenheim and Mrs. Baker playing the title role. This was a contest which excited the battle-loving public; despite the arrival of the Panama steamer both houses were packed on that night with cheering partisans of the two favorites. And Mrs. Baker triumphed, said the Bulletin of next evening, awarding the laurels to her entire company:

> "If the visitor has previously seen this piece in the Opera House, he will probably think that its representation at the Lyceum is somewhat inferior. The scenery is not quite as beautiful,nor do the actors, generally in the principal parts, approach those in the other house. Probably Miss Adelaide Gougenheim does not aspire to be considered equal to Mrs. Baker in the part of 'Pauvrette,' while it appears to us that Mr. Ryer and Mr. Booth, in the parts respectively of 'Bernard' and 'Count Maurice,' are much inferior to Mr. Baker and Mr.Courtaine in the same characters. Mr. Phelps, in the Lyceum, makes but a trifling fellow of the Republican soldier, 'Michel.'

Having thus eliminated all competition the Bakers continued a successful run of Pauvrette, a sentimental melodrama with a hackneyed plot and a pseudo-historical theme. Some idea of the play may be obtained from the Bulletin's critique:

> "Mrs. Baker rendered her part in this piece a very affecting one, and, many tears were silently shed in the theatre, as her innocence, her helplessness and griefs were successively portrayed. Her costume was not exactly that which a Swiss peasant might be supposed to wear on the approach of winter: and it might be advisable, on future representations, to wrap up, with some woolen stuff,a few square feet of her naked neck."

Shortly after they produced several other romantic

and historical dramas, such as the <u>First Exploits of Riche-</u>
<u>lieu</u> and the <u>Queen of Spades</u> in which Mrs. Woodward starred.
There was a reminiscence of their early Adelphi season when
on December 3 and 4 they performed in <u>London Assurance</u> and
<u>David Copperfield</u>. The usual mediocre farces and "extrava-
ganzas," however, were reducing the quality of the dramatic
output; these the Bakers may have considered as a sop to the
public. Perhaps they were underestimating their public
taste;they were certainly overestimating its generosity: only
four nights after their reappearance they were staging a benefit performance for Mrs. Baker, a too obvious exploitation
of the public's sentiments and finances. However the critic
was most indulgent in his reproof in the <u>Bulletin</u> of December
3, 1858:

> "After playing only four nights in the State --
> for old accounts were settled in this way years
> ago -- it seems rather early to make a special
> appeal to the public for a benefit. However
> the play is a good one--<u>London Assurance</u> -- and
> the principal actors of merit, and anyhow the
> house will doubtless be crowded."

The public had certainly been kind to the Bakers on
their first visit. Besides the fortune in profits they had
taken home with them Mrs. Baker on her farewell benefit had
received a most magnificent "diamond Magic watch";previous to
that her gifts had consisted of diamond rings, diamond watches,
diamond bracelets, and a "Silver tea service valued at $400."
The public was under no further obligation to them.

After a poor month in January the Bakers got off to

a new start in February. Baker was now again on the right
path as a manager and the public was overjoyed; on February 1
he gave them their beloved Hunchback; in the play were the
Starks, Mrs. Baker, Sophie Edwin and J. B. Booth. "He had now
a very complete,a very strong company,probably (as the Bulletin,Feb. 2, 1858 says) the best ever collected in California
up to this time." And he gave them during the month other
favorite classics: The Gamester, The Wife, Othello,with these
estimable actors.

For some reason Mrs. Baker was missing from the company during March; in her stead Baker engaged Avonia Jones.
Together they played in several of the plays the Bakers had
introduced back in 1852 and 1853, at the Adelphi: Fazio, The
Bride of Lammermoor, La Tisbe, Ion, Sybil. The performance
of Sybil was a kind of reunion: in it were playing Mrs.Judah
and Thoman, who were with the Bakers during the celebrated
Adelphi season.

On March 28 the season came to a close, and for a
month the company remained idle as Baker supervised the ren-
ovation of the Opera House. The theatre was being improved;
not only was it being made more decorative but, what is possibly more important, more comfortable -- in arrangement of
seats and ventilation. The Bulletin of April 18, 1858 was
very much concerned by this change:

> "The poisonous atmosphere infesting many of
> our public buildings, when filled by an audi-
> ence, has afforded us topic for comment on many
> occasions, and we are glad to see that in the
> alterations of Maguire's establishment he was

made an honest effort, at least, to secure an
ample supply of fresh and pure air."

The theatre had been altered and renovated and im-
proved, but in other respects things were still the same. The
cast was Mrs. Baker, now returned to the fold; Lewis Baker,
James Stark, Sophie Edwin, and the Messrs. Coad and Thoman.
Mrs. Judah was not performing in this play; instead she was
hiding away in Make Your Will, the farce which followed The
Hunchback. Between the two plays appeared a Miss Jennie
Mandeville who sang favorite ballads.

This was a period in the San Francisco theatre when
performances were inordinately long. The legitimate drama
was furiously battling with variety for its very life; it had
to offer its patrons all kinds of inducements: low prices,
swollen programs, entertainment. Thus full-length, serious
dramas and tragedies were almost invariably followed by
trivial and irrelevant farces. After the Hunchback Baker
offered, on April 21, The Merchant of Venice plus The Young
Rascal of Paris; on May 3, the Greek tragedy, Medea plus The
Loan of a Lover and The Eccentric Cosmopolitan. On May 23 at
a benefit to the Hebrew Benevolent Society the tragedy of
Romeo and Juliet with D.C. Anderson, Mr.and Mrs. Baker,Stark,
and Mrs. Judah was only one item in the programs; in addition
there were Senor and Senora Marquez, Miss Kammerer, Mr. and
Mrs. Courtaine and others appearing in "a grand olio."

This was also a period when the legitimate drama
had to compete with variety in the matter of providing

thrills, spectacles, and "special attractions." The Bakers
produced at the Opera House such "magnificent military dramas"
as The Veteran (or France and Algeria), the burlesque spectacle of Lalla Rookh, and a very pretentious melodrama by
Boucicault called The Pope of Rome. It was necessary to im-
press and overwhelm audiences, and evidently The Pope of Rome
was succeeding. Remarks the Bulletin of February 13, 1858:[9]

> "This is a fine spectacle piece which was well
> received. There are some incongruities in the
> action; but the imposing black robes of the
> priests and nuns, gilded crosses, men-at-arms,
> dirge-like music, and all that style of thing,
> made the spectators and hearers quite heedless
> of any artistic defects."

The audiences were certainly getting their money's
worth. And yet in comparison with some of the latter achieve-
ments of the Bakers at the American, these dramas seem like
quiet domestic idyls.

AT THE AMERICAN

The Bakers opened the American season on September
12, 1859 with a new melodrama, one of the most spectacular
produced thus far in San Francisco, The Sea of Ice, with
Sophie Edwin, Mrs. Judah, J. B. Booth and George Ryer. Very
little is known of this play, but the title itself sounds om-
inous. The Bulletin critic was delighted with this new trend
in the drama. In the issue of September 20, 1859 he says:

> "The grand style in which this piece has been
> set on the stage excites the highest expecta-
> tions of the future liberal course of the man-
> agement."

60

He was not disappointed by the presentation the following week, of the comedy, Extremes. This was a most "lib-
eral" production, including not only "a quadrille called
La Pyrenne...danced in the course of the play by sixteen
ladies and gentlemen" which alone was worth the price of ad-
mission -- but also says The Bulletin of September 27,1859:

> "...a satire upon men and things of the present
> day, which strikes, right and left, against the
> reigning follies. Politics, ladies' dresses,
> matrimony,model philanthropy,and kindred topics
> are all touched upon."

This was also a period of mixed bills, of opera
performed in conjunction with the regular dramatic program.
In September the Italian Opera Troupe was playing at the American; this company was followed in October by the New Orleans
Opera Troupe and a French Opera Troupe. On October 6 drama
seems to have been completely submerged under a downpour of
French music. On that day, according to the Bulletin, the
performance at the American consisted of La Pauvre Jacques by
the Baker troupe; Paer's comic opera of Le Maitre Chapelle
by the French troupe of Mme. Jeanne Feret and Mlle.Eliza
Petron; the popular chorus of Les Enfants de Paris, and the
Barcarole and Prayer from Meyerbeer's L'Etoile du Nord.

However, there were intervals of dramatic lucidity
that were also successful. The drama, David Copperfield with
Mrs. Baker as David, Mrs. Judah as Aunt Betsey, and Mr. Baker
as Micawber was a very popular piece; another was All that
Glitters is not Gold, with its amusing reference to the local

scene.

Under Baker's capable and energetic management the American, for the first time in many months, was assuming a prosperous air. Lewis Baker had a remarkable ability for recognizing public trends and acting on them; he could also secure the best acting talent in San Francisco to cooperate with him; he knew how to deal with temperamental actors; he was an excellent diplomat; he knew how to adjust his dramatic programs to satisfy the fickle tastes of the public; he gave the public what it wanted and at the same time he did not cheapen his theatre.

BAKER HUMORS A FICKLE PUBLIC

The taste for a time was for "novelties," for "special attractions" -- for "stunts." Stars like Ada Menken were calling attention to their peculiar talents by performing spectacular tours de force. This was the age of Mazeppa. A common stunt was for an actress to play a man's part in a play, or to assume several roles in one play. Mrs. Baker's talents were generally of a quieter nature, but she had to adjust herself to the trend.

On October 8 the famous sensation-piece, Dumas' The Corsican Brothers, was given with Mrs. Baker playing the principal roles, those of the brothers Franchi. Her acting in this play impressed the critics. Mrs. Baker's roles heretofore had been of the sweet, charming, gracefully feminine type;

she had been successful as the tender Juliet in <u>Romeo and Juliet</u>, the graceful Julia in <u>The Hunchback</u>, disarming as the Miss Hardcastle of <u>She Stoops to Conquer</u>, coquettish as the Constance Fondlove in <u>The Love Chase</u>. She had heretofore given no indication that she could also convincingly become a very masculine and very passionate Corsican youth; and not only one Corsican, but two! That she could do so is a tribute to an unexpected and astonishing versatility.

Spectacle followed spectacle; the theatre was striving for effect, and the public was becoming more and more responsive. They were being lured out of the variety halls in greater numbers back into the legitimate theatres. And Lewis Baker was contributing his share towards this recrudescence of the legitimate drama in San Francisco. He was having a great success at the American, almost as great as he had had six years before at the Adelphi and at the first American, and he was having success because he was reversing his original course.

In 1852 he had opened the Adelphi and had steered the drama away from preoccupation with the grandiose and the spectacular to an interest in humbler themes; in so doing he had brought the public back to the theatre. Now in 1859 he was doing the reverse: he was emphasizing spectacle; he was giving the public glamor and excitement, and again they were coming back. But Lewis Baker was an astute student of public taste; he knew that this current tendency toward the spectacular was only an expedient, a means of reawaking public

interest in the legitimate theatre. Once they had reacquired the habit of theatre-going, then more subdued, more significant plays could be interspersed with the heavily romantic melodramas.

In the meantime he was successfully producing "sensation dramas" and historical spectacles, in variety and quantity. The Poet's Wife, first presented on October 14, 1859 was followed by a pretentiously magnificent piece called The Wars of Napoleon the Great, in which the role of Napoleon was taken by George Ryer. This was followed by another romantic adventure drama, The Three Guardsmen an adaptation of Dumas' Three Musketeers, in which Junius Booth played D'Artagnan.

On November 17 the American tried to stir up interest in the drama in another way. It produced for the first time a new local drama called Gold, dealing with scenes and situations very familiar to the audience. However, this play did not have much success on successive repetitions; its chief defect, according to the Herald, (November 18, 1859) was that it was not very flattering to California miners.

Soon after, Baker returned to his spectacles: The Son of the Night, The Mormons, The Invincibles, The Veteran. The spectacles were becoming daily more spectacular, involving all the members of his company -- Mrs. Baker, Mrs. Judah, Sophie Edwin, the Mandevilles, George Ryer, D.C. Anderson, William Barry, J. B. Booth and others -- dozens of supernumeraries, elaborate and magnificent settings. But Lewis

64

Baker's inspirations had not yet dried up. In December Victoria and Albert joined the Baker troupe to play an engagement in a new and widely advertised spectacle, The Elephant of Siam. The critics found the acting of Victoria and Albert to be very convincing; the fact that Victoria and Albert were two elephants helped the realism. Victoria and Albert were very educated, but not too intellectual, and they made a hit.

Victoria and Albert were followed by Mr. and Mrs. Forbes, who had played in the East and in London. For a time at the American the audiences had a rest from spectacle as they watched the Forbes perform skillfully in such standard classics as The Hunchback, Lucrezia Borgia, and Macbeth. In the latter play, given on December 17, was a very impressive supporting cast, consisting of Booth, Ryer, Baker, Anderson, Barry, Thoman and Frank Mayo.

Soon, however, Baker was back to spectacle. The Veteran and the Corsican Brothers were repeated. New pieces were introduced, some of which were obviously intended for children, like the "romantic and magnificent" Ivanhoe produced for Ryer's benefit on December 23. Shortly after Christmas there appeared at the American a "magnificent holiday piece" The King of the Alps, a popular play based on a German legend, and involving the whole Baker company. The management had advertised it long previously as excelling "in the interest of its plot, the vigor of the action, and the gorgeous splendor of its appointments anything that has ever been introduced

in this city...a holiday treat to be looked forward to, for the young folks." (Bulletin, December 19, 1859)

Fortunately, however, the year did not end for the Bakers with any more juvenile pyrotechnics. On December 28 the Pennsylvania Engine Company, No. 12, the same brave fire-boys who had so gallantly rendered tribute to Mrs. Baker on her first appearance at the Opera House, received a benefit at the American, and on that occasion was presented, not a roaring spectacle, but a light and charming drawing-room comedy, Old Heads and Young Hearts. On the 31st Junius Brutus Booth had his benefit. This was the first time in two years this quiet and dependable actor was given the opportunity to receive due recognition; he selected for his benefit the role created by Chanfrau, "Mose" in the melodrama, A Glance at New York; but in addition he chose to play the crooked-back ty-rant of Shakespeare's Richard III. And thus the decade came to an end.

The Baker company continued to play for the next two weeks at the American. Richard III had established another temporary precedent and upon the engagement of Hackett as star they performed in other Shakespearean pieces: Henry IV, The Merry Wives of Windsor. On January 14, 1860 the season ended with The Three Guardsmen.

The American engagement had been a very successful one for the Bakers and their capable troupe. They were con-tinuing the tradition of legitimate drama in San Francisco

when all about them variety was thriving. At the beginning
of 1860 Maguire's Opera House, where the Bakers had made their
reappearance in San Francisco, had fallen victim to the trend:
it had abandoned the legitimate drama and was housing only
variety and dramatic "novelties." The American under the
Bakers was the only citadel of legitimate drama to resist the
siege of variety; they were of course forced to compromise,
but the point is this -- the Bakers for the second time had
come to the rescue of drama in San Francisco: first, when
inefficient management was bringing about its suicide;the
second time, when it was being throttled to death by an ag-
gressive variety. Each time the Bakers had nursed the drama
back to health. There was nothing spectacular about their
life or their methods. The Bakers lived and worked quietly.
In contrast to many of their contemporaries they demonstrated
that one can produce significant work without the accompaniment of clamorous shouting.

In January, after the close of the American season,
the Bakers took their docile troop to Sacramento. They were
back in two weeks to play an engagement at the Lyceum, with
Baker still stage manager and with Hackett playing opposite
Mrs. Baker in such diversified roles as "Falstaff" in The
Merry Wives of Windsor, "Nimrod Wildfire" in the comedy of The
Kentuckian and "O'Callahan" in the farce of His Lost Legs.

This was an age of hyperbole and therefore Baker
announced his next star, H. A. Perry, as "the greatest and best

living actor"; but Mr. Perry evidently did not live up to his reputation. He played the lead in <u>Much Ado about Nothing</u>, <u>Othello</u>, <u>Don Cesar de Bazan</u>, <u>Wild Oats</u>, and the <u>Merchant   of Venice</u>; he also was "Gossamer, the Laughing Philosopher" in the farce <u>Laugh When You Can</u>; "Wacousta" in the melodrama, Wacousta or The Curse; "the ultimate Pollywog"in the burlesque of <u>Metamora, or The Last of the Pollywogs</u>; and "Edward Middleton" in <u>The Drunkard</u>. But the <u>Bulletin</u> which had been getting rather critical lately of Baker's offerings at the Lyceum was not friendly to Mr. Perry; for it said,on February 14, 1860:

> "...if ranting and mouthing a commonplace con-
> ception of character be marks of a great trage-
> dian, then is Mr. Perry one. There is little
> that is graceful or noble in his bearing on the
> stage."

After this journalistic rebuff Baker went to the other extreme: he set about securing the services of the world's worst actors. There were many of them in San Fran-cisco: pitiful young men who haunted the offices of theatre managers, suffering from the sad and bizarre obsession that they were great actors. Sometimes it was considered a good joke to humor one of these lunatics,to publicize him extrav-agantly as a star in a widely advertised production. It was an immense practical joke and newspapers and audiences co-operated with glee.

A PATHETIC BURLESQUE

Early in October 1859 a certain   Mr. Defries

approached Baker and insisted that as an actor he was far superior to any one else in the country, and that he should be
engaged immediately to play Hamlet.

"Have you ever been in a play before?" asked Baker.

"Well, not exactly," hesitated Mr. Defries, "but I
can give recitations." And he promptly went into Hamlet's
Soliloquy, complete with gestures.

Baker listened to Mr. Defries with mixed feelings.
One was a desire to chase Mr. Defries out of his office, or
run very far away himself. Another was to explode with
laughter. Then an idea occurred to him: why not engage Mr.
Defries to play Hamlet, take the newspapers and audiences into his confidence, treat Mr. Defries as if he indeed were the
world's greatest actor? It would be a marvelous practical
joke, a super-sensation, a variation from the other "spectacles" of the month.

Mr. Defries was accordingly engaged to play Hamlet
and San Francisco was duly informed. The newspapers announced him as "the world's greatest actor," a crowded and
enthusiastic house greeted his debut. He had been carefully
rehearsed by the hysterical Baker troupe, was presented with
a startling costume; and Mr. Defries in turn had added a few
more gestures to his repertoire.

All week Mr. Defries atrociously mutilated Shakespeare and the audiences applauded him furiously on his en-
trance, after each speech, at the end of each scene, made him

take innumerable curtain calls.

As another Baker "spectacle" Mr. Defries was thriving famously. Then came the climax: on October 21, Mr. Defries took his benefit. The Bulletin announced:

> "Mr. Defries, who will have it that he is a great actor, will take a benefit this evening when he will appear as 'Hamlet.' He has been in this character; but he is determined to push through or die (and 'be d---d') in the attempt."

Again Mr. Defries was welcomed effusively by the audience; he strutted around in his gorgeous costume flinging his speeches and gestures about, captivating the audience. Then it began; but it was all started by Mr. Defries.

"To be or not to be --" began Mr. Defries.

Somebody threw an orange. Mr. Defries' next gesture was a disarming one: he caught the orange and without interrupting his impassioned soliloquy calmly proceeded to peel and eat it. This only stopped the audience a moment; in the next moment the air was full of assorted fruit, vegetables and weird cries. Mr. Defries' voice grew louder and his gestures more pronounced; he bravely struggled through the storm; then he saw the entire audience rise from its seats and make for him. With a series of bounds Mr. Defries was off the stage, out of the theatre, and galloping down the street, the entire audience of the American Theatre in frenzied pursuit.

Mr. Defries was never heard of again. But the sadistic audience had a fine time and Baker was always eager to present it with similar treats. On February 24 a poor

harmless maniac named C. H. De Wolf was cajoled into another Shakespearean role; De Wolf delighted the audience of the Lyceum as Shylock.

But after a while even such treats began to pall on the public; Baker began hunting for new diversions. San Francisco has always been loyal to its own artists and writers, and the Baker troupe produced a series of dramas written by local writers. One of these was an irrelevant historical drama, The Last Days of Robespierre written by "a lady of this city." Yet even chivalry could not prevent the critics from being less than enthusiastic for this drama.

Having tried almost every kind of feast to tickle the jaded public and critics without much success, Baker was obliged to return to the old familiar classics. During the early part of March the Baker stock company, composed now of Mr. and Mrs. Baker, Sophie Edwin, Booth and Ryer produced The Lady of Lyons, Damon and Pythias, Richelieu, Wild Oats, and The Love Chase. The season at the Lyceum, however, ended on April 3 with two melodramas carrying the suggestive titles of The Hidden Hand and Six Degrees of Crime.

BAKER SUCCUMBS TO POPULAR TASTE

On April 12, 1860 the Bakers began the last phase of their San Francisco career. On that date they helped to reopen the American Theatre; Baker was this time again stage manager, Booth and Ryer acting as general managers and heads of a company which featured the Bakers, Mrs. Woodward, Sophie

71

Edwin, Jenny Mandeville and Thoman. The legitimate drama temporarily revived by the astute management of Lewis Baker was now again succumbing to the onslaughts of variety; it was resisting desperately. One of the principal changes noted by the newspapers at the American reopening was that prices had been reduced one-half -- to 50 and 25 cents.

But even low prices were not enough; the management was determined to attract the audiences away from the variety houses at whatever cost to the cause of true legitimate drama. They decided that since the various local dramas, novelties, spectacles, farces, stunts they had presented to San Francisco had each had a success, a combination of all these elements plus additional elements from the rival source of variety and minstrelsy would produce a super-success. Accordingly they selected the opening of the American for the first presentation of their grandiose idea. This was a local drama with a local theme, The Three Fast Men of San Francisco, a spectacle play, featuring the Californian debut of the Yankee comedian, W. W. Allen; a company of female minstrels; and Mrs. Baker playing in seven characters and Jenny Mandeville in seven! Though everybody tried very hard the result was not entirely successful as far as the critics were concerned. Said the Bulletin on April 13, 1860:

> "The local drama of The Three Fast Men of San Francisco (so called probably because the words Stockton Street and Sacramento are occasionally spoken by the characters) is a long, dreary farce in five acts. There is no plot of the slightest interest, and the piece only shows the buffooneries of a few personages who successively

visit a gaming house, a thieves-den, a fortune-
teller parlor, a masked ball, etc. The grand
feature in the farce is the imitation, by   a
number of females, of the   negro-minstrelsy,
Ethiopian jokes, stale conundrums and Alabam'
dancing of Billy Birch and Joe Murphy's troupe.
There is a great deal of coarse animal life exhibited.   The fists are freely used, and hats
are knocked over the victims' heads, a cry   of
police,is heard and everybody runs, etc. These
things produce a laugh, but immediately afterward one is sorry that he has been tempted to
indulge in mirth at such absurdities..."

Having considered the matter thoroughly the Bulletin

a week later returned with a general denunciation of the man-

agement's new policies.   It found in their cowardly surrender

to the coarse influences of variety a   treacherous betrayal to

their public and to the cause of the legitimate drama.   Says

the Bulletin of April 19, 1860:

"We have been particularly requested by those
interested to pitch into the farce   of   The
Three Fast Young Men of San Francisco, (they
say) Anything that shows how vulgar, gross and
indecent a play it is will be sure to persuade
a San Francisco audience particularly the ladies, to visit the   theatre.   We are reminded
that the present Ryer-Baker-Booth company have
produced of late some of the finest dramas in
the English language, but they were played only
to a 'beggarly account of empty boxes.' Finding
San Francisco weary of the refined and   intellectual, the management produced the present
piece and at once crowded the house nightly and
put money in their purse.   Latterly, however,
the rush has commenced to slacken, and it   is
thought that a good sharp census of the piece
will bury it hard.   Well, we can only   repeat
that the piece is worthless as a drama,that the
management who produced it, and the actors and
especially the actresses who perform in it,
should be ashamed of themselves and their calling; that the men who persuade women to see it
cannot be their well-wishers; and that whoever
sees it, voluntarily a second time, or who sits

it out a first time unless under duress has a
taste for very low pleasures. We cannot believe that either ladies or gentlemen will pa-
tronize the American Theatre, as long as the
present management conduct their business on
the principles so dishonorable to San Francisco,
which we have been lead to believe they enter-
tain."

This was an age when prize fighters and critics did
not wear gloves; and they struck hard. This was not an age
of compromise; either the critics exalted plays and actors to
the skies or else kicked them around in the dust. Baker who
had so long enjoyed the favor of the critics had acquired no
skill at parrying these sudden blows. But he, unlike most
of his contemporaries, had a talent for diplomacy, a gift for
compromise. That was why his success as a manager was so
great. He was able to convince Booth and Ryer that they had
made a mistake and that they could start off on the right
track again by admitting their mistake.

On May 2 the Bulletin announced that the Booth-
Baker-Ryer company was beginning a new series of dramatic en-
tertainments. He was pleased to remark that The Three Fast
Men of San Francisco would be "pruned of its old vulgarities
and indecencies." On May 7 they went back to the successful
genre of the "sensation play," producing a new drama by the
prolific Dion Boucicault, The Romance of a Poor Young Woman.
The wrath of the critics had by now thoroughly cooled down;
they found the Boucicault drama to be "full of striking
'lights and shades' and...effective on the stage." (Bulletin,
May 8, 1860).

74

FAREWELL TO SAN FRANCISCO!

The Bakers had now only one more week on the San Francisco stage and in their parting gesture turned back time, returning to their first Adelphi season of 1852 -- they gave San Francisco Dickens once more. On May 14 and May 16 they appeared in <u>Oliver Twist</u> and <u>Nicholas Nickleby</u>. On the last date they received their complimentary benefit tendered by the entire theatrical profession and in a week were gone from San Francisco. They left a gap in the San Francisco legitimate drama that could never quite be filled; without Mrs. Baker's tender ministrations, without Baker's capable direction, the legitimate drama was to slump and for a time sink into oblivion.

For many years afterward the Bakers played in the principal theatres of the East, winning acclaim wherever they appeared. Finally they retired to Philadelphia, the city of their first love, and it was here they died -- Baker in 1873 and Mrs. Baker in 1887. They bequeathed to the stage a daughter, Josephine Baker, who later married John Drew of the Arch Street Theatre in Philadelphia and became aunt of the Barrymore family.

In the whole picture of the American theatre the Bakers are lost but in the pattern of the San Francisco stage their figures stand out very prominently. Twice the Bakers rescued the legitimate theatre of San Francisco; their strong hands supported the tottering structure of San Francisco

drama in the time of its greatest need. They created a theatre into which successive generations of actors and managers
could find a place. They were the pioneer actor-managers of
San Francisco.

REPRESENTATIVE PARTS TAKEN BY THE BAKERS

Date	Play	Role	
		Alexina Fisher Baker	Lewis Baker
1852	The Hunchback	Julia	Master Walter
	Romeo and Juliet	Juliet	Mercutio
	Fazio	Bianca	Fazio
	David Copperfield	David	Micawber
	The School for Scandal	Lady Teazle	Sir Peter Teazle
	She Stoops to Conquer	Miss Hardcastle	
1853	Wild Oats	Lady Amaranth	Rover
	The Critic		Mr. Puff
	Douglas	Young Norval	
	The Bride of Lammermoor	Lucy Aston	Ravenswood
	Evadne	Evadne	
	The Wife	Mariana	
	The Lady of Lyons	Pauline	Claude Melnotte
	Love's Sacrifice	Margaret Elmore	
	London Assurance	Lady Gay Spanker	Sir Harcourt Courtley
	The Love Chase	Constance Fondlove	

Representative Parts Taken by The Bakers, cont.

Date	Play	Role	
		Alexina Fisher Baker	Lewis Baker
1858	Pauvrette	Pauvrette	Bernard
	Exploits of Richelieu		Chevalier de Matignon
1859	The Gamester	Mrs. Beverly	Lewson
	Othello	Desdemona	Cassio
	Armand (or The Peer and the Peasant)		Armand
	Sybil	Eustice Clifden	
	The Merchant of Venice	Portia	Bassanio
	Medea		
1859	The Sea of Ice	Ogarita	Captain de Lescours
	Extremes	Mrs. Crosby	Smiley
	Marble Heart	Mlle. Marco	Ferdinand Volage
	Three Guardsmen		Buckingham
	The Elephant of Siam		
	Our American Cousin	Florence Trenchard	Lord Dundreary
	Henry IV		Hotspur
	Merry Wives of Windsor	Mrs. Ford	Dr. Caius
1860	Taming of the Shrew	Katherine	Petruchio
	Old Heads and Young Hearts	Lady Alice Hawthorne	Jesse Rural
	The Belle's Stratagem	Letitia Hardy	Flutter
	The Romance of a Poor Young Woman	Jane Pride	Richard Pride
	The Surgeon of Paris	Rossignol	Charles IX
	Oliver Twist	Nancy Sykes	Fagin
	Nicholas Nickleby	Smike	Newman Nogg

THE BAKERS

BIBLIOGRAPHY

Coad, Oral Sumner   Mims, Edwin, Jr.,   The American Stage Pageant of America (New Haven, Yale University Press,1929)

Leman, Walter M.   Memories of an Old Actor (San Francisco, A. Roman & Company, 1886).

Lloyd, Benjamin Estelle   Lights and Shades of San Francisco (San Francisco, A. L. Bancroft and Company, 1876).

McCabe, John H.   McCabe's Journals   (unpublished Mss.Bound Sutro Library, San Francisco).

Phillips, Catherine Coffin. Portsmouth Plaza (San Francisco, John Henry Nash, 1932).

Rourke, Constance.   Troupers of the Gold Coast or The Rise of Lotta Crabtree.   (New York, Harcourt,Brace and Company, 1928).

Soule, F., Gihon, J. H., M.D., and Nesbit, James. Annals of San Francisco (New York, D. Appleton and Company, 1918).

Young, John P.   History of San Francisco (San Francisco, Chicago, S. J. Clark Publishing Company, 1912).

NEWSPAPERS AND PERIODICALS

The Daily Evening Bulletin (San Francisco) Nov.-Dec.1858 -- Public Library, Newspaper Room.

The Golden Era (San Francisco) Dec. 1852; Jan., March, May, Nov. 1853; Jan. 1854; May, 1880, Public Library -- Sutro.

The San Francisco Herald Nov. 1859.

TABLE OF CONTENTS

THE CHAPMANS

(For dates, see Family Tree on Chapmans)

THE CHAPMAN FAMILY
(A SECTION OF THE FAMILY TREE)

WILLIAM CHAPMAN
(1769 - 1839)

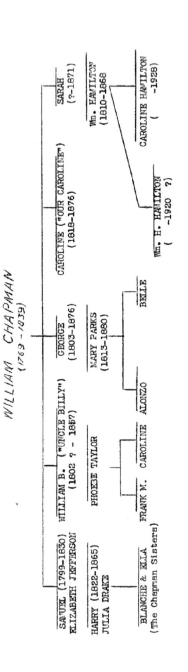

SAMUEL (1799-1830)
ELIZABETH JEFFERSON

HARRY (1822-1865)
JULIA DRAKE

BLANCHE & ELLA
(The Chapman Sisters)

WILLIAM B. ("UNCLE BILLY")
(1802 ? - 1867)

PHOEBE TAYLOR

FRANK M.   CAROLINE   ALONZO

GEORGE
(1803-1876)

MARY PARKS
(1813-1880)

BELLE

CAROLINE ("OUR CAROLINE")
(1818-1876)

Wm. H. HAMILTON
(-1920 ?)

SARAH
(?-1871)

Wm. HAMILTON
(1810-1868)

CAROLINE HAMILTON
(-1928)

CAROLINE ("OUR CAROLINE") CHAPMAN

(1818 - 1876)

WILLIAM B. ("UNCLE BILLY") CHAPMAN

(1802? - 1857)

76

THE CHAPMANS
Strolling Players on the San Francisco Stage

During the fifties it was difficult to throw a stone at a San Francisco stage without hitting one or two Chapmans. Chapmans were everywhere. They swarmed all over, singing, dancing, playing in comedy, melodrama, farce, burlesque, Shakespeare. If by some miracle all the other actors had suddenly vanished from San Francisco the Chapman clan would no doubt have been able to take over the entire theatre themselves.

The Chapmans were a unique phenomenon in the American theatre. An unusually prolific family they represented the tradition of the acting family, the tradition of the strolling players. Chapmans were born on the stage and died on the stage. There had been a Chapman who was a member of Shakespeare's company; there had been a Chapman who was the original Beggar in The Beggar's Opera. The ancient tradition of the Chapman clan isolated them from others;like gypsies they were close and secretive, with a habit of finger communication, with a private language of their own. They were

vagabond actors; it was inevitable that in 1851 and 1852 they should come to the mecca of American actors -- California.

THE CLAN

The Chapmans had not been American actors for a very long time; theirs was a European tradition. The idea of America first possessed the patriarch, William Chapman, in the late 1820's. For thirty years he had been manager of the ancient Theatre Royal, Covent Garden, in London; he had acted there, together with members of his large family, during the theatrical reign of Mrs. Siddons. About 1827 he transported his brood to America. These were his sons and daughters: Samuel, William B., George, Sarah, and Caroline; two others, Bernard and Elizabeth, remained in England.

With the facility and versatility of those born to the theatre the Chapmans could play anything; they acted in tragedies, comedies, farces, interspersing a song and dance between the acts. They were at home in every genre of the theatre, from the highest to the lowest. The theatre was their home.

In the Eastern cities and towns the Chapmans had been successful, but it was in the East that the Chapman family was beginning to disintegrate; it was difficult to find engagements which could include the whole family. William Chapman, whose heart was filled with an inexahustible love for his children, was determined to keep them together.

EASTERN DEBUTS

In 1828 William Chapman pere made his American debut at the Bowery Theatre in New York, in <u>Othello</u>. Soon afterwards, his two eldest sons made their debut at the same theatre; two years later Samuel and William B. Chapman went to Philadelphia to become the first managers of the Walnut Street Theatre. They also continued as actors. On October 3, 1829 William B. played Rip Van Winkle -- the third to play this famous role. The Chapmans were tightening their bonds with the American theatre; Samuel a short time later married Elizabeth Jefferson, the sister of Joseph Jefferson, the actor who was later to become famous as Rip Van Winkle. In later years Frank M. Chapman, the son of William B. Chapman, became manager of Joseph Jefferson -- the ties of Jefferson with the Chapman family were rather complex.

Then calamity struck the Chapman family. Riding to the theatre one day, Samuel fell from his horse and broke his leg. The doctor urged immediate amputation. Samuel,who as a child had played Prince Arthur in <u>King John</u> with Mrs. Siddons at Covent Garden and could look forward to no other life but that of the theatre, exclaimed: "Cut my leg off? Never! Rather would I die first!" And he died. The good citizens of Philadelphia who had loved him put up a monument to his memory.

It was probably this disaster which determined Papa Chapman's next step. He had to do something to keep the family together, to keep them constantly under the protective patriarchial wing. Necessity produced the first showboat.

79

THE MISSISSIPPI SHOWBOAT

In 1830 wanderlust had driven the Chapmans from the eastern cities to the small towns of the middle west. The legendary passion of William Chapman for fishing is, by many writers, used to explain the origin of the first showboat. A more banal explanation is the increasing size and unwieldiness of the Chapman family. It was very difficult to find halls where they could perform; it was difficult to find hotels where they could sleep. Troupers were often stranded in the little towns and it was difficult for them to find transportation.

One afternoon (so the story goes) while Chapman pere was sitting on the bank of the Mississippi with a fishing pole in his hand, he saw a flatboat floating downstream and that gave him the idea -- Floating Theatre!

And so the showboat, with its flag projecting above a side roof bearing the single word "Theatre," with its comfortable little house forward, its little hall with wooden benches and tiny stage with muslin curtains and tallow candles for footlights, floated with the current, from town to town, up and down the Ohio and Mississippi Rivers. Here the Chapmans lived and here they played.

It was a kind of idyllic existence where they put on plays for their own amusement, worked at a large repertoire, played in classic tragedy, danced, sang, acted in blackface. But mostly they fished. Acting and fishing

were the great interests of their lives, and there was much overlapping. They learned their parts with a book in one hand and a pole in the other, and often during intermissions and while offstage they would run out, throw over a line, and see how the fish were biting.

RIVER LIFE

Dozens of amusing anecdotes are told about the Chapman craze for fishing and how this sometimes interferred with the coherence of their dramas. Once while performing in The Stranger, one of the favorite dramas of the period, this revision of the usual scene (Scene 1, Act IV) occurred:

"The Stranger: (calling his servant) Frances!
Frances!   (No reply)
Frances!   Frances!   (Pause)
(angrily)   Frances!

Distant Voice: Coming, sir! (Considerable
pause. The Stranger walks up
and down in a towering rage.)

The Stranger: Frances!   (Enter Frances)

Frances: Here I am, sir.

The Stranger: Where the d--? Why did you not
come when I called?

Frances: Why, sir, I was just hauling in a nine
pound catfish...But you should have
seen the one that got away.*

It was said that even after leaving the showboat, the Chapmans smelled almost constantly of fish. Usually the fish bit quite freely, but sometimes, for the struggling

---

*Theatrical Management in the West and South, Sol.F. Smith.

81

Chapmans there was not even fish to eat. In lieu of money for
tickets they were often glad to accept vegetables, eggs, and
poultry. The audiences were sometimes very poor, if not critical, and the Chapmans had to be content with what they got.

They stopped at every town or village on the banks
of the river, throwing out a gangplank wherever there was the
possibility of an audience. They did their own billing,
tacking the programs to neighborhood trees. They were also
their own musicians. These were the days when music was a
necessary prop for melodrama; it was used to produce all kinds
of emotional effects. The Chapmans had no real orchestra,
but they themselves played all the necessary music behind the
scenes. Whenever an actor or actress came on there was always the proper chord. The "frontwood robber," dressed in
topboots, face buried in inky whiskers and wig, would deliver
himself of his villainous schemes confidentially to the audience to accompaniment of violins played pizzicato. Everybody
died to slow music; sometimes it was very inconveient when
the actors doubled as the musicians. In one play Harry
Chapman, who was first violin and was also playing in a stark
tragedy, received his fatal sword-thrust and proceeded duti-
fully to expire. He staggered to the wings and fell with his
head and shoulders off stage, spoke his last speech, and
played slow music for himself as he died. The Chapmans were
remarkably ingenious.

Those early days on the Mississippi were full of

delightful incident, reflecting on the growing popularity of the showboat. Captain Louis Rosche in "Old Man River" relates one adventure in his aggressively popular dialect:

> "One time before Chapman had his steam packet, he tied up his barge theatre at some little old one-horse town where mostly everybody was as poor as a church mouse and couldn't raise the price of admission, which was fifty cents. A crowd of them wanted to see the show, though, and hung around all afternoon trying to get him to give 'em a cut rate. But he wouldn't do it and went ahead with a performance for a handful of people who had enough money to get in.
>
> "The rest of them hung around on the wharf feeling like a bunch of children somebody sent to bed without any supper, and when they heard the folks inside the barge laughing and clapping their hands, that was too much for them. So they cut the ropes and gave the boat a shove, sending it down the river. Everybody on the inside was so busy either acting or watching the show, none of 'em had any idea what was happening and the boat floated on down the stream five or six miles before it fetched up on a sand-bar. When the show was over and the audience found out they had to wade ashore, they were hopping mad, and I reckon Mr. Chapman had to do some tall talking before he made 'em see it wasn't his fault." (San Francisco Examiner's American Weekly, March 20, 1938.)

In a few years the showboat had become a permanent institution on the Mississippi and the Chapmans had accumulated enough money to buy a small steamboat which they fitted up very comfortably as a theatre with a pilot, engineers and deck hands. For eleven years, between 1830 and 1840, "Chapman's Floating Palace" plied up and down the Mississippi. Here they acted, here they lived, loved, were born, married, died. Especially born -- for the Chapmans had extraordinary vitality and fertility.

83

THE TRIBE INCREASES

In March, 1838 Sarah Chapman and William Hamilton, an Englishman who had just joined the company, came down the gangplank together at Jackson, Mississippi, and returned to the showboat as man and wife. On the Chapman Floating Palace a large family was born. What with the original family, the marriages, the intermarriages, the Chapmans soon had enough actors to cast even the fullest of Shakespearean tragedies.

Also married on the boat was George Chapman; he too married a member of the company, a widow called Mary Parks. Mrs. George Chapman later gave birth to an interesting family of twenty children; she survived all but three of them.

William B., the eldest son of William Chapman, had married in England Phoebe Taylor, a musician who later became the first organist of St. Mary's Cathedral on California and Dupont Streets in San Francisco. They had two sons.

In 1840 old Mr. Chapman played his last part and caught his last fish. With his death the idyllic existence of the showboat came to an end. Without the patriarch to hold them together the Chapman family quickly scattered.

CAROLINE AT BURTON'S

Caroline, the youngest, never married. In time she became known as the most gifted, the most versatile, the most popular and famous of the Chapmans. She was only 22 when she

went to New York with her brother William B., but she had
been brought up on the showboat, had acquired amazing stage
resources and an expanding reputation as an exquisite dancer,
an enchanting singer, an actress equally proficient in tragedy, comedy and burlesque. Although not beautiful, she had
an amazing charm and personality, so that later San Francisco
took her to its heart possessively and called her "Our
Caroline." Says Constance Rourke in _Troupers of the Gold
Coast_:

> "Not beautiful, in repose she seemed awkward,
> but she had through experience gained a wide
> expressive range. Her plain features took on
> radiance, her dark eyes flashed, her lank fig-
> ure melted into grace. With vivacity she could
> play low comedy, burlesque, sing mock Italian
> bravura, impersonate Mrs. Bracebirdle in _The
> Tragedy Queen_ with something of Covent Garden
> splendor...."

At Burton's Theatre in New York Caroline became almost instantly famous. In _The Annals of the New York Stage_,
Odel quotes Ireland, the critic, as calling her "the most
vivacious soubrette known to our stage." He praises her "versatility, almost unprecedented" and her work in low comedy
"not only entirely unsurpassed, but nearly unrivalled." Her
style was "perfectly original" and her chambermaids and rus-
tics were "totally free from stage conventionalities." In
melodrama she "invariably brought down the house in thunders
of applause." He described her physical appearance:

> "Though her features were plain, her large mouth
> was redeemed by the whitest of ivory, and her
> lustrous dark eyes could convey a glance more

meaning, of either mirth or sadness, than any
contemporary optics on the New York stage."

Critic Ireland wondered how she could have attained
such stage ability in the crude theatres of the West, in her
father's "floating establishment on the Ohio and Mississippi
Rivers," and how she could have remained so long unknown to
New York.   But it was the hard school of the showboat that
gave Caroline the necessary experience, that sharpened her
talents.   At Burton's she was the whole show; she was the
"Famed Caroline Chapman of Burton's"; she made for the immense
popularity of the theatre and the wealth of the proprietor.
After her triumphs at Burton's, Caroline played a season at
the Olympic, a "branch" establishment.

BARNUM ENGAGEMENT

Then she joined Barnum -- after all, with her amazing talents she was something of a freak!   However, she was
not exhibited in a cage, but in Barnum's Stock Company at the
American Museum.   Caroline played in that perennial American
classic, The Drunkard.   The critics were shocked at what they
termed this debasement of her talents, at her "spending the
winter as companion to beasts and birds in the so-called Happy Family of the Menagerie."*

Acting with Caroline was her brother, William B.,
known primarily as a low comedian although he too could at a

*Annals of New York Stage, Vol. VI p. 71

moment's notice slip into any part which demanded the talents of a singer or dancer or tragedian; and her sister Sarah Hamilton who, like Caroline, was plain of face but known as a fine tragedienne.   In 1852 this branch of the Chapman family journeyed across the continent to California; but another contingent of the Chapmans had preceded them by about a year. In 1850, under the management of Charles R. Thorne, the "George Chapman Family" had arrived in California; they were among the very first of San Francisco pioneer actors.

THE GEORGE CHAPMAN FAMILY

The outstanding member of the George Chapman family was unquestionably Mrs. Chapman.   In 1850 she gave a performance with her husband, her daughters Clara and Josephine, in a hall on Washington Street; but since it was difficult to get a good company together they soon left for Sacramento. Here they opened a theatre.   One night during a performance word came that a hospital was burning; Chapman led his company to the blazing building and they carried the occupants to his theatre.   Mrs. Chapman wrapped the patients in the silks and velvets of her stage wardrobe, went home and wrote an account of the fire for the Alta California. She was also a contributor to the Golden Era. Besides being an actress and writer she also found time to raise an amazing number of children.

As the George Chapman family continued to expand, the problem of finding a suitable cast no longer occurred.

87

Their repertoire was constantly increasing, embracing all the
current standard dramas and popular comedies, high and low.
The sole problem was to find theatres for their performances.
With the prevalence of fires this was a difficult task.

CALL OF THE NOMADIC LIFE

The Chapmans however did not have to remain in
cities; they were essentially strolling players and were much
happier when they could lead a nomadic existence. In 1851
they left Sacramento for a tour of the mining regions. They
were the first accomplished actors to make the tour. They
traveled all through California, Washington, and Oregon. The
life was never too rough for them and they received an enthusiastic welcome from the miners. This kind of life ap-
pealed to them and for many years they continued to travel
through the mountains, with occasional brief incursions into
the city. In October 1851 the George Chapman family suddenly popped up in San Francisco. Their previous engagement
had had its effect and they were cordially welcomed.

With Junius Booth, Jr., George Chapman opened the
American Theatre. On October 22 they made their debut in
the Lady of Lyons. Mrs. Chapman played the role of Pauline,
apparently a standard choice for debutantes in San Francisco
-- it had also been the part selected by Mrs. Baker and Mrs.
Stark for their first appearances. Mrs. Chapman, playing
opposite James Stark, produced an immediate impression, which
was augmented by succeeding performances in the following

days in the comedies <u>The Honeymoon</u> and <u>The Serious Family</u>.
The critics remarked on the sprightliness of her acting; comedy was evidently Mrs. Chapman's forte, as it was that of the
other Chapmans. But like all Chapmans, she was not limited
to one theatrical genre. During the first week of November
she played such diversified roles as Calanthe in <u>Damon and
Pythias</u>, Jack Sheppard in the play by that name, the title
role in <u>Therese</u>, Juliet to Stark's Romeo, and Minnie in <u>Some-
body Else</u>.

The ostensible head of the George Chapman family
was completely subordinate to his wife:he had to content himself with the sobriquets "Honest George," or"Good Old George";
he was respected by San Francisco as a "good citizen." His
daughters, Mary and Josephine, and Clara Rivers were more esteemed by theatre-goers; they were charming dancers and
pleased the audiences with their polkas, hornpipes, and tarantulas. Also rising in popularity was his eldest son, Alonzo,
showing much promise as an upholder of the Chapman comic tradition. When he played with his mother and Stark as Peter in
<u>The Stranger</u> on October 30 the critic of the <u>California Cou-
rier</u> discovered in him "considerable ability and comic effect."

On November 16th the Family made their last appearance at the American and quickly scuttled off to the
mines. At the end of January they were back at the American.
After a month or two, during which time Alonzo had arrived
at such proficiency that he could be entrusted with a leading

role, (in My Neighbor's Wife) performed for the first time on
January 29, 1852) they were off again.   The wandering troupers   were not again heard of until a year later   when, during
January and February, they   played an   engagement   at the San
Francisco Hall.   This   terminated with a magnificent benefit
for   Mrs. Chapman; like almost all the other actresses of the
time she was adored by the   woman-starved   population   of San
Francisco.   Reviewing this benefit the Golden Era of February
13 said:

MRS. CHAPMAN'S POPULARITY

"The   complimentary   benefit given to this lady
on Thursday   evening   last, was, without doubt,
the   most   brilliant affair   yet   witnessed   in
California.   The   demonstration was   not gotten
up   for   the   purpose of ascertaining who would
pay the highest   price for an hour's amusement,
or to give the votaries of fashion an opportunity for   displaying   the   beauties   of 'codfish
aristocracy,' but for the purpose of testifying
the kindly feelings which are   entertained   for
one who   has   been   among us for several years,
and who, with   a large   and interesting family,
intends to settle   in one   of our own beautiful
valleys, where   the   wages of   her professional
labors   will   be expended   for the adornment of
our young State, to the prosperity of which she
has so long   been identified.   'Success to the
Chapman Family.'"

Mrs. Chapman   did not disappoint   her well-wishers;
she did settle in California.   Long after deserting the stage
she continued to live   in   San Francisco, until   her death in
1880, surviving her husband   by four years, as well as seven-
teen of her   twenty children.   Her most prominent bequest to
San Francisco was her daughter, Belle Chapman, who became one

of the most important members of the celebrated California
Theatre Stock Company. With her husband and with many others
of the Chapman host Mrs. George Chapman is buried in Lone
Mountain Cemetery.

But in 1853 Mrs. Chapman was very much alive. In
February with the Family augmented by several other competent
actors she was giving performances in Marysville. We next
hear of the Family in May of the same year when they darted
again into San Francisco and took over once more the American.
This was a brilliant and colorful season of drama and comedy
featuring Mrs. Chapman in farce with George Chapman, and exotic dances by the Chapman girls.

For their opening performance on June 22, 1853
they selected again one of their favorite comedies, The Honeymoon, in which Mrs. Chapman appeared as Juliana; the farce,
The Artful Dodger, with George Chapman as Tim Tinkle ; and
popular dances by Mary and Josephine Chapman. Comedy, farce,
and ballet continued to constitute the Chapman bill of fare.
The next week (May 29, 1853) they put on the "serio-comic
drama," The Serious Family, in which the entire Family participated; the farce, The Wheelwright; and the Spanish dance
La Jota with the Misses Chapman and Rivers.

June was a brilliant month for Mrs. Chapman. On
the 5th the Family produced the "grand Eastern spectacle" of
The French Spy which apparently was a tour de force for the
talented actress. In announcing the play, The Golden Era of

91

June 5, 1853 was very flattering:

> "Mrs. Chapman will appear as the heroine,
> 'Mathilde,' a character in which she certainly
> has no rival in California. Mrs. G. Chapman
> will appear as 'Mohammed,' and the talented and
> promising Alonzo in the character of 'Tony.'
> We have frequently witnessed the performances of
> The French Spy in the largest theatres in the
> East, but were never more pleased with the de-
> lineation of the bold and devoted 'Mathilde'
> than by Mrs. G. Chapman, on the California
> boards. In the combat scene with 'Mohammed,'
> she displays a skill in fencing which would do
> credit to a professor of the art, and which
> never fails to call forth the heartiest ap-
> plause."

The month continued with the performance of many
favorite comedies, dramas and farces, such as Crasher and
Slasher, The Lottery Ticket, Nicholas Nickleby, Jack Sheppard,
The Artful Dodger; and many graceful dances, plain and fancy.
The San Franciscans were becoming increasingly more devoted
to Mrs. Chapman; they displayed their affection, as usual, by
their response at benefits. On June 26, 1853 there was a
benefit at the American for her, "a whole-souled lady and an
excellent artist." The fact that the Family had been so long
in California and appeared to be considering it as their permanent residence after a career of wandering over the country,
drew from the Golden Era (of June 26) this moral:

> "Our playgoers should learn to discriminate be-
> tween those who have 'driven their stakes'
> among us, and those who, Shylock-like, hoard up
> all the gold that comes within their grasp and
> who, when the ostensible object of their mis-
> sion is attained, leave the country and laugh
> at those who -- (to use the language of one of
> them) were foolish enough to pay so dearly for

the acting of broken-down melodramatic ranters
and diabolical low comedians, whose genius in
the East commanded the enormous sums of $6 to
$8 per week."

The San Francisco public was beginning to turn
against the actors who had so cruelly exploited its sentiments. Even such favorites as the Starks and the Bakers had
turned out to be fortune hunters, leaving San Francisco as
soon as they had accumulated a fortune, to try their luck
elsewhere. By contrast the public appreciated the loyalty of
a Mrs. Judah who remained in San Francisco, fair weather or
foul; the constancy of the Chapmans who, after a lifetime of
wandering, were content to pass the final phase of their career in California.

For the next few months the Family continued successfully at the American. But soon the blood of the strolling actors, which flowed so turbulently in their veins, bore
them away from their admirers. October found them back in
the mountains, continuing their successes in the mining towns
of San Joaquin Valley, in Columbia, Sonora, Marysville. Again
and again the Family were to dash into San Francisco for
brief visits, after their trips through the mountains, until
finally the miners began to be bored and the San Francisco
welcome wore out.

In July, August and September of 1853 the San
Francisco public displayed its appreciation of their talents
by staging benefits to almost every member of the huge Family.

93

On August 2, 1853 the young danseuse Mary Chapman received her testimonial; for this occasion a guest comedian, Charles A. King, joined the company to play the role of Bob Smithers in The Model Farm, assisted by Mrs. Chapman as Lotty Smithers. On September 18, "Honest George" Chapman was given his benefit. The next evening was a special benefit for the beloved Mrs. Chapman. The burlesque of Beauty and the Beast was given. This was indeed a special event in the life of the Chapmans; it was the important occasion of a family re-union, for joining with the Family in their celebration were San Francisco's "Uncle Billy" and "Our Caroline" Chapman.

UNCLE BILLY CHAPMAN

William B. Chapman was called "Uncle Billy" by George Chapman's children; it was inevitable that the idea would catch on with the other half of San Francisco. He was an uncle to everybody and when he died in San Francisco in 1857 his thousands of friends throughout the country mourned his loss. He died like a true Chapman, practically on the stage; although old and broken he was active to the last. A month before his death, on November 7, 1857 he was perform-ing at Maguire's Opera House as Alphonso in Delicate Ground and O'Smirk in The Dumb Belle. The obituary in the Bulletin of November 9, 1857 thus summed up his career in San Francisco:

> "Mr. Chapman was the best low comedian in this State. His humor was natural and overflowing. No audience could resist sympathizing with his mirth. His first step on the boards was the

signal for a general smile; and as he opened
his mouth, his hearers burst into laughter. He
was a most useful man to any management, prepared at the shortest notice to take any part,
from the lover of twenty, "sighing like a fur-
nace," to the lean and slippered pantaloon. He
would sing, dance, and fight with those who
were young enough to be his grandchildren. He
was never at a loss before the footlights; if
he did not know or had forgotten the author's
words, or cared nothing for them--which was often enough the case--he gave his own, which if
not so classical as the original were pretty
sure to raise a grin on every face. The liber-
ty of gagging--mother's 'tolerable, and not to
be endured'--was forgiven in 'Uncle Billy.' He
was a universal favorite and will long be re-
gretted by lovers of drama in this State."

ADVENT OF CAROLINE AND WM. B. CHAPMAN

In 1852 William B. Chapman arrived in California
with his sisters Caroline and Mrs. Hamilton to whom he had
been closely attached ever since leaving the showboat. On
March 15, 1852 he made his debut at the Jenny Lind Theatre as
Dr. Pangloss in the comedy, Heir at Law Mrs. Hamilton assisted him as Lady Duberly. Although usually eclipsed by
his more brilliant and spectacular sister, Billy Hamilton
rapidly built up a substantial reputation as a character actor; now, because of his increasing age he was specializing
in old men's roles; Dr. Pangloss was one of his favorite
parts.

Like all the Chapmans, he too had within him a remarkable flair for comedy, which usually veered to the burlesque. He was a master of what is known as "low" comedy:
he could play the clown, he could sing, he could dance, and

was a marvellous entertainer. He was in the habit of "throwing the audience into convulsions with the comical songs in his cornucopia of whimsicalities" (Herald, June 16, 1853) or "with his inexhaustible fund of anecdotes keeping the house in a roar from the rise to the fall of the curtain." His talent was fundamentally inclined toward farce but he had the versatility of his family; he very easily slipped into such roles as Grumio in Katherine and Petruchio, Tony Lumpkin in She Stoops to Conquer, the First Gravedigger in Hamlet, and Duke of Gloster in Richard III.

The last role, however, was some kind of a joke, probably a burlesque. Performed on the occasion of his benefit at the American (November 28, 1856), together with the fourth act of the Merchant of Venice, in which his son played Shylock, the audience was instructed that "no cabbages will be allowed on the stage, they not being characters in the play." This benefit was a characteristic Chapman riot: besides the excerpts from Shakespeare there was the comedy, Breach of Promise, songs and dances, and "Our Caroline" delivering the hunting speech from London Assurance.

BILL AND CAROLINE AT THE JENNY LIND

On March 24, 1852 Caroline Chapman made her debut at the Jenny Lind; she appeared as Widow Cheerly in the comedy, The Soldier's Daughter, and Beauty in the extravaganza, Beauty and the Beast. The critics admired her "pleasing and graceful" manner, and a week later Caroline delighted

them with one of her "graceful dances." From then on she entranced her audiences with the brilliance and fecundity of her talents. She flashed before them in Shakespeare, in farce, in the old English comedies. During the next 'two weeks she was Lydia Languish in The Rivals, Lucille in A Story of the Heart, The Spy in The French Spy. Meanwhile Uncle Billy with spontaneity and verve kept up a running patter of songs, conundrums, recitations.

Nothing was too lavish or pretentious for the Chapmans to undertake. They followed the spectacle play, The French Spy, with the grand musical spectacle of Clari, Maid of Milan, the lavish burlesque tragedy, Bombastes Furioso -- and then they were gone from San Francisco to play a short engagement at Sacramento. In May, however, they were back at the Jenny Lind, full of inexhaustible energy, putting on more exuberant, more extravagant productions. The Naiad Queen was followed by The Fair One with the Golden Locks and the spectacular Green Bushes.

CAROLINE, THE VERSATILE

But the Chapmans were too sensible to continue dazzling their audiences with spectacle. They often offered more solid drama, such as Dombey and Son (July 12, 1852), comedies, such as The Review (May 18), and a local farce, A Trip to California, (July 11). Uncle Billy continued to send the house off into gales of laughter with his comic acting. As Paul Pry he was especially successful. Like many of his

roles, this was a slapstick part, "a character which he rendered with great fidelity and spirit, now popping in at malapropos moments, now tumbling into the window, chased by a pack of dogs, always with his invariable old umbrella. . ." (Alta California, July 19, 1852.) And Caroline interspersed her more serious roles with her exhilarating dancing, with her enchanting songs. Her "Sweep Song" was becoming the theme song of the Jenny Lind, and was hummed all over San Francisco. Caroline continued to startle her audiences with the diversity of her talents; this was an age of tours de force and during July she performed very often in the celebrated farce, Actress of all Work, in which she took five different characters. Out of the Chapman cornucopia flowed every conceivable delight.

THE CHAPMANS WITH THE BOOTHS

At the end of July there was great excitement in San Francisco. The strange, quixotic genius, the great tragedian, Junius Booth, had arrived in town and was playing a two weeks engagement at the Jenny Lind. With him were his wife and his young son, Edwin. The two great acting families joined forces for this special event. It would seem the walls would burst as San Francisco packed the Jenny Lind to watch "Our Caroline" playing against the magnificent Booth. Just a while before, the audiences had been delighted by extravaganza, easily pleased by shabby farces. Now they listened intently and in a sober silence to the tortured grandeur

that was the elder Booth.

On July 30, 1852 Booth made his first appearance as Sir Edward Mortimer to Caroline's Helen in the _Iron Chest_, that powerful drama that was Booth's favorite in San Francisco. It was an interesting combination: the lyricism and lightness of Caroline against the somber, tragic background of Booth. Constance Rourke make her own analysis:

> "Caroline Chapman played with a natural grasp of the essentials of character within which her strange native passion could overflow, but she had cast away nearly everything of fixed tradition she had ever known. The elder Booth played within a ritual, essentially simple, by which every touch of action or of business had long since been prearranged. If the mold seemed rigid, there was beauty--or might be--infinite revelations of character. Within that deep pattern a wild and transcendent life might burn, as if by the renouncement of small individualisms an inner understanding could be made complete."*

They played together, the Chapmans and the Booths, in _Othello_, _Hamlet_, _Macbeth_, _Richard III_, _A New Way to Pay Old Debts_. This was the real debut of Edwin Booth; it was also an occasion when a few of the younger members of the Chapman dynasty made their official entries on the stage. Frank M. Chapman, the son of Uncle Billy, appeared in a child's role with Booth; William H. Hamilton, the nephew of Uncle Billy, appeared as the boy, Fleance, in _Macbeth_; his mother, Sarah Hamilton, played Lady Macbeth, and the Booths took over the other principal roles; Junius Brutus

*_Troupers of the Gold Coast_, pp. 43-44.

99

Booth as Macbeth, Junius B. Booth, Jr., as Macduff, and Edwin Booth as Malcolm. Caroline danced, Uncle Billy sang comic songs; they played together in a farce. It was altogether a field day for the Chapmans and the Booths.

CAROLINE AND BILLY IN THE MINES

In the autumn of 1852 tne Jenny Lind had been sold to the city by Maguire to be converted into a city hall; the Booths were dispersed; the Chapmans were off to the mines.

It was a kind of life which pleased these hardy troupers; in it was a constant element of danger which spiced their existence. San Francisco was possibly becoming too tame for these vagabonds. In the San Joaquin Valley there was cold and rain; there was the constant, entertaining possibility of bandits; life in the camps was full and riotous. They played in every camp, large and small, in bars, in tents, in flimsy hotels. Everywhere they were received with a giddy and passionate enthusiasm.

When they arrived at Columbia they found a real theatre to receive them. Columbia, one of the largest camps in the mountains, had sprung up over night into a real city. Its theatre had been built by an actor who, arriving in San Francisco when ships were being deserted wholesale by the gold-crazy sailors, had by use of his dramatic wiles terrorized the crew into unloading his ship. For a season this nameless actor joined the Chapmans. The Chapmans had to depend upon accidental meetings with other strolling actors

GEORGE   CHAPMAN

(1803 - 1876)

and amateurs for the formation of their company. But they
played with everyone, played everything.

FAVORITES OF THE MINING CAMPS

In December when they opened the Broadway Theatre
with an actor called Campbell, producing the old favorite,
Beauty and the Beast, they started a riot. The overjoyed
miners threw buckskin purses crammed with nuggets, onto the
stage. They followed the Chapmans to and from the theatre
at every performance, often carrying them gayly on their
shoulders. On succeeding nights they bombarded the stage
with such a flood of coins that the region was completely exhausted of silver until spring.

There was a freedom, an extravagance, a spontaneity
about life in the mining camps; the Chapmans could do anything they liked; the miners welcomed every new outburst of
dramatic frenzy. When they left Columbia for the opening of
the new Phoenix Theatre in Sonora on New Year's Eve, a mob of
miners, a thousand strong, formed their escort. In Sonora,
Caroline spoke the opening address on the little stage in
back of the saloon. She sang, Uncle Billy played the banjo
and cracked jokes. They produced an enthusiastic She Stoops
to Conquer. During the next week they put on Theresa, or the
Orphan of Geneva,The Hunchback, The Hundred Pound Note, Betsy
Baker, and other popular favorites of the time, with the as-
sistance of an occasional amateur and with their companion-
able sister and brother-in-law,the Hamiltons.Then they played

in Campo Seco, and in February were back in San Francisco.

"OUR CAROLINE" AT THE SAN FRANCISCO THEATRE

At the San Francisco Theatre the Chapmans and the Booths were reunited. On February 18, 1853 Caroline, Billy and Hamilton joined Junius Brutus Booth, Jr., in taking over the management of the theatre. Soon that pioneer entertainer, Dr. Robinson, joined the company, to sing his own songs, recite his own verses, and play in his own plays. Then young Edwin Booth joined them, after a winter of hardships in the mountains. Edwin Booth's talents as the potential great tragedian were not yet recognized. He had to strum a banjo, play the lead in The American Fireman, spread burnt cork on his face in a blackface version of Box and Cox, and burlesque local celebrities.

As a comedian Edwin Booth was never much of a sensation. Even in tragic roles his future greatness was not yet seen; it took the more discerning critics of the East to "discover" him later. On April 21 he played Richard III to Caroline's Elizabeth (no comment in the newspapers). Two days later, on his benefit, he played Hamlet for the first time; Caroline played opposite him as Ophelia and Billy was the First Gravedigger. Of this performance the Alta California (April 26) had only this to say:

IN SHAKESPEAREAN ROLES

"Miss Chapman's Ophelia, of course, was excellent as everything is which this most talented

woman undertakes."

Of another later performance as Ophelia the critic
of the _Herald_ (June 15, 1853) had this to add:

> "Her representation of the beautiful, confiding
> and unfortunate lady was so effectively render-
> ed, so true to nature, as to draw tears to the
> eyes of her audience. The versatility of this
> admirable actress is astonishing. In tragedy,
> in comedy, melodrama and burlesque she appears
> equally at home, and in all natural, piquant
> and attractive."

And indeed the spring of 1853 at the San Francisco
Theatre was a fecund and glorious period in the career of
Caroline Chapman.   It was just before Lewis Baker was to
start his career as a manager in San Francisco and to inaugu-
rate a new trend in drama, insistence on more thorough rehearsals; more finished performances.   But now there was a
new play every night and whether the lines were well learned
or not did not make much difference -- there was plenty of
enthusiasm.   The Chapmans romped about in comedies, high and
low, all kinds of farces and burlesques, tragedies, Shakespeare, musical extravaganza.

During April, 1853 Caroline cavorted about tire-
lessly in such a bewildering variety of performances as the
opera _Guy Mannering_ (April 6), _Richard III_ (April 21),   the
extravaganza, _Yellow Dwarf_ (April 22), the fine old English
comedy of manners, _The Rivals_ (April 23), the spectacle _Green_
Bushes (April 24).   With all the copiousness of her talents
Caroline's modesty is refreshing; there is something quiet
and unassuming in her gaiety, in her sprightliness, a certain

graceful off handed charm. At the height of her career the
Daily Alta California (December 7, 1853) thus analyzed her
charm, with the inevitable moral:

> "It is no disparagement to any other actress we
> have ever had in California, to say that in her
> particular role of characters, she has never
> had an equal. In either genteel or low comedy
> she by far excels all others,and it matters not
> whether singing,dancing, or acting is required,
> she is equally proficient in all, and brings
> the highest cultivation and most graceful na-
> tive qualities to the performances. The clear,
> happy laugh and the perfectly natural noncha-
> lance appear so simple and unaffected that out
> of pure sympathy her audiences must enjoy the
> play. She evidently loves and takes pleasure
> in her profession. In heavy tragedy she does
> not essay to rank with several others, and she
> therefore does not appear in parts of higher
> character. It may be said of her that she
> never appears but with a glad smile for her au-
> dience, and that she never fails to receive in
> return a similar welcome.
>
> "Of her merits, there is, so far as we know,
> but one opinion, and all pronounce her excel-
> lent. Of others, even the best, there is a
> variety of opinion, and some object to one
> thing and some to another, but of Miss Chapman
> nothing is said but in way of approbation. She
> quietly pursues her way, affording unmixed
> pleasure to her audiences; and with no loud
> flourish of trumpets, no mammoth play-bills to
> announce a reappearance, she labors on to the
> satisfaction of a public that seems to think
> that the only thing entitled to support and
> complimentary benefits is pretension. With all
> Miss Chapman's merit and her long residence in
> California, she has hardly ever been honored
> with a complimentary benefit. Yet repeatedly
> we have seen densely packed houses when some
> awkward amateur was to appear, whose proper vo-
> cation was that of an oyster rather than an ac-
> tor. But so goes the world. Sound and fury
> are the things that win, and not merit. 'Tis
> so on the stage; 'tis so everywhere."

104

CAROLINE AND LOLA MONTEZ

In June, 1853 the glamorous Lola Montez fluttered into San Francisco self-consciously encumbered by a gaudy past, brocaded with romantic legends. Everybody was appropriately excited by her autobiography, shocked by her dancing, bored by her acting. But the notoriety of her character threatened to steal the public away from the San Francisco Theatre; and Caroline, the star, accepted the challenge. She threw down her gauntlet.

Lola played in Maritana, taking three parts; Caroline topped this with the perennial little burlesque, The Actress of All Work, playing seven parts in twenty minutes! Lola produced her autobiographical play, Lola Montez in Bavaria; immediately afterwards the Chapmans introduced a short extravaganza with the same title, which had been a success in New York. Flinging all her theatrical stock away, Lola produced a serious historical drama, Charlotte Corday, in which she tried to identify herself with the eighteenth century revolutionist; she danced two spider dances in one evening; at a fireman's benefit she gave selections from all her plays.

Although this tour de force exhausted the ingenuity of Lola Montez, it did not tax the cleverness of the Chapman troupe. They relentlessly continued to persecute the fabulous Countess with their travesties. The critics and the public knew that they had something even more devastating up

their sleeves; they held their breaths and expectantly await-
ed the next move.   It came during the final week of June,
1853.

THE CHAPMAN - MONTEZ FEUD

On June 26 another of the Chapmans joined the feud.
At the American Theatre, young Mary Chapman danced the Spider
Dance.   This, according to the boisterous critics, was much
better than the original -- in fact, "knocked the socks off
the fiery Countess." (Golden Era, June 26).   And then, over
at the San Francisco Theatre the other Chapman branch put on
a new local burlesque, a full length extravaganza by Dr.
Robinson called Who's Got the Countess? Full of satiric allusions and personal innuendo, ridiculing the arrogance and
pretense of Lola Montez, this burlesque aroused a storm of
protest.   The critics began to battle among themselves and
found everything wrong with the play itself.   Said the Alta
California of June 25:

> "The plot of the piece -- if it may be called a
> 'plot'--is very miserably arranged, and the di-
> alogue lacking in wit, point, appropriateness
> and even in common sense, and is, to crown all,
> bunglingly arranged in bad rhyme."

The next day the Golden Era appeared in violent
disagreement: it congratulated Dr. Robinson on producing the
first successful original piece in California.   But they ac-
cused Billy Chapman in his "Spider Dance" of "laying it on a
leetle too thick."   According to the Alta, this dance and
Caroline's acting were the only redeeming features of the

play.

The critical feud waxed hot; readers wrote indignant letters to the editors, adding fuel to the flame. One such reader, carried away by an impetuous gallantry wrote a letter full of picturesquely eloquent prose, to the _Herald_ (June 26, 1853) calling upon all of Lola's loyal public to defend the honor of their besmirched idol, and lamenting the lady-like Caroline's lowering herself by indulging in rude and ugly personalities. Some of this passionately oratorical letter deserves quotation:

> "With the exception of Miss Chapman's comic bravura, and Mr. Chapman's grotesque dance, which after all are the great points in the burlesque, but which would be equally amusing if entirely disconnected with it, the whole affair is an exceedingly coarse and vulgar attack upon one who, whatever her faults and foibles may have been, has proved herself a noble-hearted and generous woman, and who little deserves that her exertions in behalf of suffering humanity, so freely offered, so readily accepted, should be paid by ridicule and scurrility. Who is there that, after serious reflection on the character and conduct of Lola Montez while a visitor among us, can go and witness with pleasure and delight a vulgar misrepresentation of her manners and behavior, a ridiculous caricature of her person and a coarse exaggeration of her peculiarities? Not you, gallant firemen of San Francisco, of whom she spoke with so much heartfelt enthusiasm, and to whose noble charity she so finely and voluntarily contributed thousands of dollars. Not you, members of the Benevolent Association, for whom she toiled with so much pleasure, well knowing that the wide spread of your charity was not confined by prejudices of race or religion--not you, or those who through you, have become the gratified recipients of her bounty. Not one who possesses a particle of taste, a spark of chivalry, or a feeling of sympathy for

an unprotected but lovely, generous and confiding woman, in his composition....

"Such performances as the "Spy-Dear Dance,"
though sufficiently nonsensical, are at any
rate legitimate sources of fun, and occasionally exceedingly amusing. But a lady! Gentlemen
--a lady! If no gratitude is felt for her be-
nevolence, good taste should have decreed at
least that her name and character should not be
publicly ridiculed and outraged in this commun-
ity. But besides all this, there is another
stringent reason why this effort of genius
should not have been placed before the public.
There probably never was, and never will be,an
actress in San Francisco who has made more warm
friends and admirers than Miss Caroline Chapman.
She can play anything and everything and do it
well, and her name is an unfailing attraction
wherever she appears. No matter what she undertakes, she renders herself acceptable, and generally far more than acceptable, to her audience. If she were to play the 'Devil,' I
haven't the least doubt she would do it perfectly, and be greeted with roars of applause; but
we don't want to see her in any such character.
Miss Chapman is a lady, and a most admirable
artist; and I cannot believe that lowering her
in this manner to a more profound depth than I
have supposed low comedy to be capable of, can
be more agreeable to herself than it is to her
admirers. 'It's really not at all in her way."
No! NO! We've had enough of this; personalities may amuse for a moment, but a little reflection makes them offensive. Give us 'Beauty'
again, charming Carry, and don't let them make
a Mule of you any longer."

Yet, though critics railed and flung broadsides at

one another, at Dr. Robinson, at the Chapmans; as the editors

continued to be bombarded with angry epistles, some less elo-

quent but all equally inspired; the San Francisco Theatre

continued to be crowded at every performance. Lola Montez

was of course popular, but San Francisco also had a sense of

humor. It laughed at Caroline's impersonations of Mula,

the stormy actress who never knew her lines, stamping, co-
quetting, whirling through the ridiculous ballet of "Spy-
Dear!" It laughed at Uncle Billy's clowning through the role
of Louis Buggins. Even the sober Booth got into the spirit
of the burlesque with his ridiculous Plunkitt. Gradually
as the enthusiastic public demanded more and more repetitions
of Who's Got the Countess? Dr. Robinson kept building up the
piece, including more and more characters until everybody in
the cast of the American Theatre -- where Lola had been playing -- was in it: the manager, the critics, the prompter,
even the audience! When, on June 25, Caroline played Juliet
to Booth's Romeo, Romeo and Juliet was preceded by the bur-
letta, Who's Got the Countess?

For weeks at the San Francisco Theatre hilarity
reigned; Lola Montez was completely routed by a more brilliant, more accomplished actress. Gracefully Lola submitted
to the defeat and retired from the field. Soon she abandoned
San Francisco, taking with her a new husband, a certain
Patrick Hull, possibly a salve to her injured feelings. And
she was gone.

LOLA HEAPS COALS OF FIRE

But this was not the last time Caroline and the
colorful Countess were to meet as theatrical enemies. Again
in 1856 Caroline, now in her decline, was to struggle desperately against a waning popularity with another burlesque of
Lola Montez, A Trip to Australia or Lola Montez on the Fanny
Major.

109

Against the Chapmans, however, Lola dismissed all
thought of personal animosity. While the theatre represented
to Caroline all of life, to Lola it was but a small fragment
of her complicated existence. She accepted the presence of
Caroline Chapman in the stock company at the American Theatre
when she played an engagement there in 1856. Testifying to
her innate good nature and her affection for children is a
little garment -- now preserved by the California Historical
Society -- knitted by Lola Montez and given by her to little
Caroline Hamilton, the namesake and niece of Caroline Chapman.

THE HAMILTONS

Little Caroline Hamilton has some kind of historical importance as the first child actress to play Little
Eva in Uncle Tom's Cabin in San Francisco. In October, 1867
at her father's benefit at the Metropolitan she made her
debut as a full-grown actress, playing Julia in the old favorite, The Hunchback. Her Chapman blood, her father's care-
ful training stood her in good stead. The critics had lost
their earlier flair for rhapsodic over-statement, but they
were favorable to this new Chapman. Said the Alta California
of October 14, 1867:

> "Miss Hamilton has a fine appearance, good
> figure, graceful action, and excellent mem-
> ory; her correct memory was noticeable in the
> perfect reproduction of her tutor's style of
> emphasis and hesitation, to her own detriment
> at times. If the instructor could have giv-
> en the idea of the character, without these

effects, the debut would have been a wonderful success; such abandon and profuse gestic-
ulations certainly never before were at the
command of a novice, and used with such good
effect. Some of the points fell short of
the effect intended, because of the slow
approach of the climax, the opposite extreme
being the usual fault of beginners. With study
in a correct school, Miss Hamilton will be a
great addition to the stage."

Caroline Hamilton, with all her brothers and sisters, had been born on the Chapman showboat. Consequently
they all in time became accomplished and versatile show
people. Their mother, Sarah Hamilton, had a fine reputation
as a tragedienne, being especially successful in the roles of
Lady Macbeth and Queen Elizabeth. In the Chapman Collection
at the California Historical Society is the crown she wore as
Queen Elizabeth. The Hamiltons came to San Francisco with
Caroline and Uncle Billy and for a time acted with them, although they were sufficiently numerous to form their own private branch of the Chapman dynasty.

The Hamiltons played at the Jenny Lind, the San
Francisco Theatre, Maguire's Opera House, the Metropolitan
Theatre -- William H. Hamilton in most cases assumed the role
of actor-manager. Little is known of his acting ability, although he was probably quite proficient as a result of his
experience in London and on the showboat and at Burton's in
New York. The California Historical Society Quarterly (Vol.
VII, p. 282) reports that "he was said to be a quiet, unassuming man who possessed an inexhaustible fund of general in-
formation and was greatly esteemed by all who knew him."

111

With his family, Hamilton remained in San Francisco until 1859. They then traveled through the South until the Civil War broke out and forced them to return North. After short engagements in New York and Philadelphia they came West once more. In 1868 Hamilton sailed to Europe for an operation for cancer and died in London. His wife, Sarah, like most of the California actresses, was of sturdy stock. She survived her husband until 1871. Like her sister-in-law, Mrs. George Chapman, she also outlived most of her numerous progeny. Two children who survived her became well-known on the San Francisco stage: Caroline Hamilton, who lived on until 1928, and William H. Hamilton, who died at the age of eighty-three, and who among other things had taken the part of the boy, Fleance, in a production of _Macbeth_ in 1852 at the old Jenny Lind in which the entire Booth family participated; he had also in the course of his adventurous career been a pony express rider for Wells-Fargo between Reno and Virginia City.

CAROLINE AT THE AMERICAN

After practically making a career for herself as a parodist of Lola Montez, Caroline with characteristic zest swerved off into other fields. In July and August, 1853 she was playing with Uncle Billy in such classics as _The Rivals_, _Katherine and Petruchio_, _Much Ado About Nothing_, and _The Merchant of Venice_. Then on August 23, she plunged into a new local extravaganza by the exuberant Dr. Robinson, _The Past, Present and Future of San Francisco_. Like most of Dr.

112

Robinson's literary productions this was in remarkably atro-
cious verse but it was full of sprightly local allusions and
delighted the audience. Caroline appeared as "the Genius of
San Francisco" in no less than ten different disguises. The
Herald of August 24 was pleased with her performance, although ambiguous about the nature of the play:

> "Her admirable mimicry in the scene of the
> Music Girl was particularly well received and
> gave a very truthful idea of a remarkable fu-
> ture in the Past and Present, and in all prob-
> ability, the Future of our City."

On September 19, Caroline and Uncle Billy volun-
teered their services at a benefit for brother George at the
American Theatre, and soon were out of the city. In October
they were playing at Marysville and at Stockton. Then in
December they were back again in San Francisco. On December
5 they brought light and laughter again to the darkened
American, opening with the Bakers in a production of Faustus.

This was Caroline's debut in the role of Adine
and she was so successful in her interpretation that the company was forced to repeat Faustus several times. This spectacle play became at once popular; the mise-en-scene was very
impressive, and probably had much to do with its success.
Says the Herald of Dec. 10, 1853:

> "Each representation of the legendary drama of
> Faustus improves on the preceding one in the
> manner in which its remarkable changes of scen-
> ery are executed, and its machinery now works
> smoothly and evenly, presenting its beautiful
> tableaux with their most imposing effect. The
> excellent acting of Mr. and Mrs. Baker and Miss
> Caroline Chapman appear to more advantage also,

as the mechanical portion of the representation
is improved, and presents altogether a combination of dramatic talent and scenic display that
is seldom equalled on any stage."

All through December Caroline performed at the
American, playing in farces, burlesques, comedies, and an occasional tragedy. On December 23 she had her benefit and for
the occasion romped gracefully through "a variety of comedy,
farce, and fairy extravaganza." Two days later, on Christmas
day, she ended her season at the American and darted off
again to the mountains.

The same evening Caroline departed from San Francisco there occurred an event of extreme importance. It was
the opening of the Metropolitan by Catherine Sinclair, inau-
gurating a new era for the San Francisco theatre. A new period was setting in, a period of glamour and sophistication
in the theatre; San Francisco was becoming urbane and cultivated; it required a glamorous setting for the personalities
of its theatre. The period of the strolling players, the
gypsy troupers, was now passing. The Chapmans were beginning
their decline.

WITH LAURA KEENE AND CATHERINE SINCLAIR

While Uncle Billy continued in San Francisco, con-
vulsing the audiences of the American in his favorite character of Billy Lackaday, Sam Slop in The Rake's Progress, and
Paul Pry -- Caroline remained in the mountains, deferring
her return to San Francisco, probably aware of the new theat-

rical trends and the changes in the Chapman fortunes.   Meanwhile, during the first few months of 1854, she strolled
through the mountains, being greeted effusively by the miners,
meeting interesting and romantic bandits, prancing about with
her old energy on the impromptu stages in the saloons of mining towns. . .For a brief moment in May she reluctantly abandoned this carefree life, and returned to San Francisco to
play with Mrs. Sinclair at the Metropolitan.   But this was
for only one evening, May 19.   The Chapmans, Caroline and
Uncle Billy, joined the   regular Metropolitan company in a
production of the popular comedy, The Serious Family, and at
the close were applauded with a suggestion of the old furor.
Caroline bowed gracefully and Uncle Billy made a facetious
impromptu speech which promptly bowled the audience out into
the aisles.   The next day they played at a benefit for Laura
Keene, the popular actress-manager of the American Theatre.
They were joined by their sister, Sarah Hamilton, and they
played Lydia Languish, Bob Acres, and Mrs. Malaprop" in The
Rivals to the complete satisfaction of a cordial audience.

            These, however, were only isolated occasions. There
were too many competing attractions in town and their welcome
quickly wore off. The Chapmans did not receive another engagement until June 29, when they became members of Laura
Keene's company at the Union. On August 2, Laura Keene abruptly departed for Australia. Again the Chapmans were stranded.
With Laura Keene, however, they played a colorful, spirited

season and revived for a time their former popularity.

CAROLINE AS BURLESQUE QUEEN

Caroline again demonstrated her startling versatility in Boucicault's comedy, A School for Scheming; in the spectacle-play, The Sea of Ice; in the broad burlesque, Williking and his Dinah. Caroline showed that in the field of burlesque she probably had no peer in the country. Her buoyancy and high spirits were contagious, creating an atmosphere of refreshing and spontaneous gaiety. On July 19, there was a new extravaganza, Taming a Tartar, which particularly delighted the Union audiences. During the performance Caroline sang and danced and accompanied herself on the hand organ -- the audience, carried away by the spirit of things, proceeded to throw quarters on the stage, and the little tambourine girl scrambled about under the shower picking them up, and the show ended with the audience dancing in the aisles and singing Caroline's "Sweep Song."

During August, 1854 there were no theatres to receive the Chapmans and they were idle; but at the end of the month Catherine Sinclair added them to her troupe at the Metropolitan. In rapid succession, starting with her first night on August 25, Caroline plunged into such formidable roles as Calanthe, the Queen, and Martina in the solid dramas of Damon and Pythias, Richard III, and Don Caesar de Bazan. She played until January 8, 1855 with the Booths, with Mme. Montplaisir, with other celebrities. She gave

abundantly of her talents but she was no longer the indefatigable Caroline of a few years before -- she was tiring.   She
had led a pace that could not be kept up indefinitely.
Caroline could no longer prance through a full length play,
an afterpiece, several entr'actes of singing and dancing in a
single evening.   The Chapman life had been too grueling.
Now the Chapmans were actually on the decline.
After Caroline left the Metropolitan on January 8, 1855 she
did not receive another engagement in San Francisco until the
end of August.   In the meantime she toured the mines once
more with her brother, but even the miners were bored.   When
they returned to San Francisco to play at the San Francisco
Theatre they found that their houses were diminishing, that
minstrelsy had erected a solid bulwark forcing them into decline.   But Caroline had resources; she was a veteran; with
her family she had weathered every gale. She came forward to
meet the competition of variety in a manner explained by
Constance Rourke, in Troupers of the Gold Coast (p. 117):

> "Presently Caroline Chapman, who had been a
> brilliant Lady Teazle,who could play an ardent,
> enchanting Juliet, in spite of her high, gawky
> stature and plain appearance and her years, who
> had at her command a more extensive repertoire
> than any actress who had appeared on the Cali-
> fornia stage--the defeated Miss Chapman sought
> to meet minstrelsy on its own ground, and came
> out in Uncle Tom's Cabin, blacked up as Topsy."

CAROLINE AS TOPSY

It was on September 3, 1855 at the San Francisco
Theatre that this striking event occurred.   It was a great

success. Uncle Billy also applied burnt cork to his face and
became Phineas; Junius Booth, Jr., was Uncle Tom; Caroline
Hamilton was Little Eva; and Uncle Tom's Cabin was given six
successive performances.   On the 10th the clamor was so great
that Little Eva's death scene was repeated after the production of Love's Fetters, on the same bill.

Caroline and Uncle Billy no longer possessed their
early unflagging energy, yet, possessed by some desperate
force,they sought to repeat their former triumphs. On September 2, they revived the play in which Uncle Billy had made his
San Francisco debut, as Dr. Pangloss in Heir at Law; also
Caroline's famous tour de force, Actress of all Work,in which
she played six characters.   The preceding evening they had
given Buckston's comedy, Leap Year or Lady's Privilege, together with another favorite farce, The Hundred Pound Note,
in which Caroline played the dual role, The Lady and the
Peasant Girl.

BACK TO THE MINES

On September 10, Caroline ended her engagement at
the San Francisco Theatre.   It had been a hectic season and
some of Caroline's early popularity had been revived; now the
Chapmans were once more off to the mines, the last round.
They were approaching the end of their high powers.   They
were going to the mines not because they wished to, but because San Francisco was weary of them.   They continued to
pour out an interminable variety of pieces in rapid succes-

sion, because that was what was demanded; the audiences demanded excitement and gayety and novelty; the Chapmans were
being worn out.

In 1856 old Uncle Billy was approximately 54 years
old and looked a decade older; even gay Caroline was no longer young -- she was 38. They had spent a lifetime on the
stage, almost always together, and now as they toured the interior of California they offered an immense repertoire. It
was a kind of second wind which inspired them. In Sacramento
they played a brief engagement and among other pieces produced
Julius Caesar; Civilization, a new European play; Hercule,
the Huron, a naturalistic spectacle play; Mohammed; Louis XIV;
and an extravaganza entitled First Night or the Virgin in
California, which had to do with an amateur actress behind
the scenes and involved a manager, a prompter, stage carpenters, actors, lamplighters in clashes and counter clashes.
First Night was followed by an opulent afterpiece, Midas.
This new vitality of the Chapmans was a burst of desperation.

RENEWAL OF THE FEUD WITH LOLA MONTEZ

In August, 1856 a tremor rocked the buildings and
sent a quiver through the inhabitants of San Francisco. It
was not an earthquake but quite an upheaval -- it was that
woman, who during her lifetime had become a legend, Lola
Montez, back from Australia and parading through the streets
of the excited city. New legends, gaudy, romantic and myster-
ious, further embellished her; her spider dance was forbid-

den in Melbourne; an actor called Folland was drowned en route
under very strange circumstances. Firm, bold, fearing no one,
the notorious Countess opened on August 7 at the American
Theatre, walking straight into the warring camp. San Francisco
held its breath. The Chapmans rolled up their sleeves; for
Lola's enemies, back from the mines, were now in control of
the American.

The Chapmans warily waited for Lola to make the first
move. The audacious Lola accepted the challenge -- she had
apparently not learned her lesson from the battle three years
before; perhaps her experience in Australia had given her re-
newed confidence in her histrionic ability. At any rate
soon she was playing the part of Mrs. Chillington in The
Morning Call with Uncle Billy Chapman opposite, and the critics were noting the remarkable improvement in her acting. The
public swung enthusiastically over to the side of Lola.

THE CRITICS' REBUKE

Imperturbably the Chapmans waited their chance.
Suddenly, on an off night for the star, they put on the old
burlesque, Lola Montez, Caroline playing the part of Catherine
Koper. But this time something went wrong. Lola Montez
had too much of a lead; the tide now turned against them. The
critics turned upon the Chapmans their most potent weapon --
silence. The Chapmans staggered -- but they had gone through
too much to be vanquished by this blow. Again they sat back
and waited for the next move on the part of their adversary.

MRS.   GEORGE   CHAPMAN

1813 - 1880

120

Soon it came.   Lola Montez announced a public auction of her jewelry for the benefit of Folland's two children. There were diamond bracelets and rings galore, rubies, jeweled crosses, pendants, a jeweled comb, lockets, necklaces, heavy pieces made of Australian gold.   This charitable gesture met with much approval -- but not from those unregenerate enfants terrible, the Chapmans.   On the eve of the auction they produced a brand-new burlesque, occuping the entire evening's bill, A Trip to Australia, or Lola Montez on the Fanny Major.

Lola's   concern for her agent's children, her charity and her spiritual interests, were pure, unmitigated hokum, thought the Chapmans -- they spent the entire   evening proving it -- and the   critics fell furiously upon them.   Yet in spite of the critical thunderbolts the Chapmans continued the burlesque, slashing vigorously and hilariously at Lola's new pose of la soeur de charite, filling the play with all kinds of imaginative detail about the Australian tour and poor Mr. Folland's death. The critics raged and the audiences howled; they filled the house every night. The entire company of the American joined the Chapmans in this festival of mirth. The cast was as follows:

```
Lola Montez, Countess of Landsfeldt  C. Chapman
Rhoda, her friend..................Mrs. Burrill
Mrs. Fidides......................Mrs. Campbell
Ella Fidides......................Fanny  Howard
Tomlinson.........................   Mr.  Coad
Simons............................  Mr. Glover
Tommy.............................  Mr. Chapman
Neptune...........................   Mr. Hann
```

The Chapmans were superb -- everybody admitted that

-- but they were most unfair, said the critics. The critics
pretended to ignore them, but they did this quite badly. Their
critiques aroused interest and curiosity, such as the one
found in the Bulletin of September 2, 1856:

> "The piece as a literary composition is not
> worthy of criticism. The subject being some-
> what notorious, and the buffooneries of the
> actors, excited much spasmodic laughter. The
> dog, the monkey and Mr. Chapman without his
> pants, were natural and very amusing."

WANING POPULARITY

In spite of the downpour of critical scorn the
Chapmans stubbornly continued the play through the fall of
1856. For a brief moment they had returned to their old
heights. But soon even their loyal public began to desert
them; they were playing to rapidly diminishing houses. With
the exception of the new burlesque, the bills at the American
lacked the old Chapman variety. They repeated the old plays.
They began to appear more and more irregularly. Finally on
December 28, 1856 they ended their American engagement and re-
ceded from the San Francisco scene. Lola Montez remained in
the ascendant; to her the final victory, for Lola was soon
to leave San Francisco and to accumulate richer and more di-
verse legends and finally to blow out in a burst of glory,
while the Chapmans slowly, slowly, were to come to a bitter,
pathetic end.

THE END OF UNCLE BILLY

The end of Uncle Billy was not long in coming. After the close of the American season he had gone once again

to the mountains, but a frenzied competition had developed in
the mining camps, and he was defeated by younger, fresher
talent.   In despair he returned to San Francisco, and finally in May, 1857 secured an engagement at the Metropolitan
where he with his sister Caroline were in support of Annette
Ince.   On September 14, the tottering old man, making his
last feeble tour of the camps, was run over by a buggy at
Marysville.   He was only slightly hurt, but this was the
shock which precipitated the end.

Two months later, in the midst of a minor engagement at Maguire's Opera House, the beloved old man died on
November 26, 1857.   The newspapers guessed his age to be 70
or 74 although he was not much over 55, but he looked exceedingly old and worn after a lifetime of unending activity,
of dancing, of singing, of joking.   For him San Francisco
felt the affection ordinarily retained for their favorite actresses.   He was very dear to them; he was "Uncle Billy."
The newspaper comment is significant of the esteem in which
this old actor and pioneer comedian was held.   In the Herald
of November 9, appeared this tearful obituary:

"It is with exceeding pain that we record the
death of W. B. Chapman, the distinguished and
veteran comedian and meritorious citizen.   Mr.
Chapman was ill for two weeks, previous to his
demise, but nothing fatal was apprehended until
just previous to the close of his mortal career.
On Saturday night, his wife was sitting at his
bedside reading to him, when the old gentleman
passed away with the quietude of an infant drop-
ping into repose.   As an artist Mr. Chapman had
no equal in his time in California; as a gentleman, he was kind-hearted, urbane, abstemious,

and a most worthy member of society. After
passing through the trying and chequered scenes
incident to his profession, in a long life of
nearly, or quite, seventy years, during which
he played in almost every portion of our vast
country, and always commanding the warmest applause and esteem of his audience, in an in-
finitude of characters, this accomplished veteran of the drama has been gathered to the
great army of the dead. The dark curtain of death
has shut him out from the stage of life...

"We shall never again behold his familiar form
and speaking features in this world; his well-
known voice and merry glance will no more address themselves to our senses, but his image,
and the remembrance of his many admirable
qualities will long remain deeply graven in
the hearts of his hosts of friends and admirers in this State and elsewhere. The void on
our stage, occasioned by his death, will probably not be filled in years, if ever."

The next day came the funeral and further lamenta-
tions:

"The cortege was quite large, and composed of
all the members of the dramatic profession in
this city and nearly all those of the French
Dramatic Company, besides many warm, personal
friends and admirers of the deceased. The
funeral of this veteran was no hollow show,
but the solemn attestation of sincere friends
to his worth and talents, and their unaffected
grief at his loss. Mr. Chapman was probably
the oldest living actor on the American or
English stages, and has been the instrument of
imparting much of gratification and innocent
enjoyment to thousands upon thousands in
England and America. That man who spends
sixty out of the seventy-four years of his
life in making the heart glad, and without
giving one pang to his fellow beings is indeed
worthy of admiration. May the 'sods of the
valley' rest lightly on the good old man."

Uncle Billy had made several fortunes during his
long career on the stage, but it appeared that there was
nothing left for his widow and orphans. William Chapman came
from a long line of impecunious vagabond players. He had

had a lot of fun out of the theatre, and that was his reward. To his dependents he left a small piece of property on Telegraph Hill, heavily mortgaged -- the house in which "Uncle Billy" used to give his famous dinners to the theatrical colony on the Hill and afterwards ride down the precipitous slopes in his rickety mule cart.

But the San Francisco theatre and the San Francisco public were not going to forget their debt of gratitude to Uncle Billy. The Eastern comedian, J. P. (Yankee) Adams, who had played with the Chapmans and had been a good friend of Uncle Billy, suggested a benefit. On November 26, a huge complimentary benefit was staged at Maguire's and at the American Theatre in which the entire theatrical profession, American and French, participated, and the proceeds were presented to the widow and orphans of William Chapman.

Even two years later San Francisco had not forgotten their beloved Uncle Billy. On April 4, 1859 as Mrs. W. B. Chapman prepared to leave for the East, she was given a grand complimentary benefit at the American for herself and her children. Participating in the show were other relatives of the late William Chapman, namely Mr. and Mrs. Hamilton, and Caroline Chapman. Shortly afterward the Hamiltons departed; and Caroline, after procuring fewer and fewer engagements and having no longer any family ties to hold her in California, reluctantly left San Francisco.

125

THE END OF CAROLINE

The Chapmans were a strongly united family and between Billy and Caroline, who had been so close together, the bond was especially strong. Caroline had never married; the only love she knew was for her brothers and sisters and for the theatre. She had seldom been separated from Billy; the stage and Billy had been so closely associated for her that it was hard for her to act with anyone else. Caroline's whole world was crumbling.

From force of habit she continued to appear on the stage, but her old vitality was disappearing. And the theatre itself was changing; was demanding, instead of the versatile troupers who were so important, a manifestation of the early days of the San Francisco stage, more specialized performers, more glamorous personalities. Caroline had had to make rapid adjustments to the change of taste, but now age and weariness were taking their toll; she no longer possessed the gift of giving the people what they wanted. She had given an impetus to the free, untrammelled theatricals that were evolving into the all-conquering variety, and she herself was submerged by the change.

During 1858 and 1859 she continued to play sporadic engagements at Maguire's Opera House and at the Lyceum, supporting such stars as "Yankee" Adams and Mrs. Wood. In 1859 she sailed East, remembering her early success at Burton's when she was the talk of New York, hoping for engagements she

was destined not to find. New York, too, had grown up; it no longer offered a welcome to the gypsy trouper. And after more than two years of disappointment Caroline returned to San Francisco.

ADVERSITY FOR CAROLINE

The end for Caroline was long-drawn and tedious. In San Francisco she knew only obscurity and illness, small parts at benefits or in minor productions. Occasionally she might be given a leading role; but it would usually be an inexpressibly bad play. The state of the drama was falling low in San Francisco. A typical example is the exaggeratedly supernatural Faustian hocus-pocus "sensation drama" called Death, or the Angel of Midnight, given on December 23, 1861, the first play in which she starred after her return to San Francisco. The deliberately casual manner in which the critic of the Bulletin discusses the plot of this terrifying drama is amusing, and merits quotation:

> "This is a tale of German diablerie. The scene is at Munich. Dr. Bernard (Mr. Thorne, Jr.) a young physician of great skill, saves many patients but profits little, pecuniarily, by his practice. He is tempted to serve others, and sell his conscience, but refuses. When in despair, the Angel of Midnight (Miss Chapman) appears before him, and they make an unholy bargain together, that whenever the said Angel shall be visible (to the Doctor only) at the couch of the sick, he (the Doctor) shall no longer use his professional talents to defeat Death, but quietly yield the struggle; for which good service, the Angel promises to give him (the Doctor) wealth, reputation, and the possession of his beloved. Many characters

mingle in the drama, and the Angel now and then
appears, of course. At last the shadow of
Death threatens the bride and the mother of the
young physician. He is in agony, and beseeches
the Angel to take his own life, but spare those
dear to him. The difficulty is finally got rid
of by prayer to Him in whose hands are the is-
sues of life and death; the Angel disappears,
the compact is broken, and the young Doctor, his
bride, his mother and the other good and indifferent characters are preserved -- the bad ones
having been previously destroyed. All this is
wonderful and terrible, and that is just what
the author intended and what the audience are
supposed to be pleased with. The villain of
the piece is the Baron de Lambeck (Mr. Mayo);
and the chief funny man is 'Dr. Rouspeck, a
Charlatan' (Mr. Thoman)"

Caroline was no longer in demand as a singer or
dancer but she continued to play in the various old favorites,
sensation plays, extravaganzas, farces, naturalistic dramas,
and fairy spectacles that were desperately offered to dazzle
the public and lure them away from the temptations of variety.
In February, 1866 she was a member of the American company
that combined with the Buislay family to produce a "grand romantic fairy spectacle" called The Elves which seemed to be a
precursor of Billy Rose's most extravagant nightmares; for
The Elves was "a medley of tragedy, comedy, farce, pantomime,
operetta, with a sprinkling of Harlequinism and a faint suggestion of the circus." (Bulletin, Jan. 22, 1856)

Caroline's engagements became more and more scarce.
In 1869, after an absence of three years from the stage, she
made her reappearance at the Alhambra; then she played a pit-
ifully small season of one week. She reappeared at the Metropolitan for one week, in August 1870. During the fall of

the year she dragged herself on a shabby tour of the interior of the State. Finally on May 5, 1876 she died in San Francisco, old beyond her years, alone and forgotten.

"THE CAROLINE CHAPMAN"

San Francisco was considerably removed from the excitement of the Civil War but at times there were brief echoes of the long thunder rolling throughout the country. At one time a little gun-running Confederate brig dashed audaciously from the bay and swept out into the sea, evading pursuit. It was a bold and defiant gesture that stirred the imagination. This little brig was called the Caroline Chapman. For Caroline Chapman too had been bold and free, lawless, disrespectful of power and pretension. She had influenced a new mood of rebellion in the theatre; had given impetus to the lawless theatricals that were now dominating the San Francisco stage, and in the change she too had been swept aside with the others, discarded to make way for the new.

The Chapmans were a great force in the development of the San Francisco theatre; they were for a time representative of San Francisco itself, the pioneer and worldly San Francisco, loving pleasure, living richly, gayly, a gypsy city enlivened by gypsy troupers, strolling players.

THE CHAPMAN SISTERS

With the disintergration of the Chapman family and

the fading of Caroline Chapman ends the story of the strolling players in San Francisco. But there is an epilogue:--

It was late one afternoon in the late seventies, when a heavily-laden stage coach clattered through the California mountains. As it curved around the road adventure was awaiting, in the form of highwaymen. There were a pair of these gentlemen, extravagantly dressed in the mode of the time; their faces were covered by black silk masks; their pistols glistened heavily in the dying sun. The bandits looked romantic. And efficient. Promptly the stage-coach stopped.

It was obvious that here was something more than a practical joke -- these people meant business. The driver flung his arms up in the air and almost fell off his perch. Inside the coach was much tremulous agitation. The sterness of the bandits relaxed as they examined the contents. They bowed gallantly as they helped descend the twittering, brightly-costumed young ladies. A few of the passengers were indignant; they fretted, they fumed; they told them that they would be late for their engagement. They did not attempt to deny that this was the troupe of the Chapman Sisters.

Chapman Sisters? The older bandit was incredulous. He remembered Caroline, and Uncle Billy, and Josephine, and

_____

*From C. Rourke, Troupers of the Gold Coast, p. 228

and George. But these had passed away. And here were these
two charming girls, Blanche and Ella Chapman. It was too
good an opportunity. The bandits cleared a space beside the
road. They shot a few times into the dirt. Everybody began
to dance.

For hours the company danced and sang on that impromptu stage, Jake Wallace ran through the interminable
stanzas of his ballad, The Days of Forty-Nine, a ventrilo-
quist tremblingly recited his patter, the Chapman sisters
danced polkas and tarantulas and chirped their merry songs.

Then the fastidious bandits buckled on their pistols and danced quadrilles and lancers with the ladies of the
company. And at the end of that, as was the chivalrous custom
of the day, they kissed each lady separately. It was romantic and democratic, and everybody had a fine time.

The bandits were very grateful for the entertainment. They helped the Chapman sisters into the coach. The
older man was especially tender. Twenty-five years before in
Sonora, he explained, he had applauded Caroline and Uncle
Billy.

The stage-coach rolled on; from the road the bandits waved a picturesque farewell. The horses galloped at a
terrific pace through the passes as the perspiring driver
furiously whipped them on. Then, after about twenty break-
neck miles, he fainted. The two Chapman girls rushed to his
side.

The driver came to, but he would not leave his seat. For under it was a treasure-box containing a fabulous sum in gold. Wells-Fargo had been saved.

And also the honor of the Chapman family, thought the Chapman sisters, Blanche and Ella.

REPRESENTATIVE PARTS TAKEN BY THE CHAPMANS

Date	Play	Role	
		Mrs. George Chapman	Mr. George Chapman
1851	The Lady of Lyons	Pauline	
	The Honeymoon	Juliana	
	The Serious Family		
	Damon and Pythias	Calanthe	
	Therese	Therese	
	Romeo and Juliet	Juliet	
	Somebody Else	Minnie	
1852	My Neighbor's Wife		
1853	The Artful Dodger		Tim Tinkle
	The French Spy	Mathilde	Mohammed
	Nicholas Nickleby		
	Jack Sheppard		
	The Model Farm	Lotty Smithers	
	Crasher and Slasher		
	The Lottery Ticket		

Date	Play	Caroline Chapman	William B. Chapman
1852	Heir at Law		Dr. Pangloss
	Katherine and Petruchio		Grumio
	She Stoops to Conquer		Tony Lumpkin
	The Soldier's Daughter	Widow Cheerly	
	Beauty and the Beast	Beauty	
	A Story of the Heart	Lucille	
	The Rivals	Lydia Languish	
	The French Spy	The Spy	
	Clari, Maid of Milan		
	Bombastes Furioso		
	The Naiad Queen		
	The Fair One With the Golden Locks		
	Dombey and Son		
	The Iron Chest	Helen	
	Theresa, or The Orphan of Geneva		

Representative Parts Taken by the Chapmans, (Cont.)

Date	Play	Role	
		Caroline Chapman	William B. Chapman
1852	The Review		
	A Trip to California		
	Actress of All Work		
	The Hunchback		
	Betsy Baker		
1853	Richard III	Elizabeth	Duke of Gloster
	Hamlet	Ophelia	First Grave Digger
	Lola Montez in Bavaria	Catherine Kloper	
	Who's Got the Countess?	Mula	Louis Buggins
	A New Way to Pay Old Debts		
	Romeo and Juliet	Juliet	
	The Merchant of Venice		
	A School for Scheming		
	The Past, Present and Future of San Francisco	The Genius of San Francisco	
	Guy Mannering		
	Faustus	Adine	
	Yellow Dwarf		
	The Rake's Progress		Sam Slop
	Much Ado About Nothing		
1854	The Serious Family		
	The Rivals	Lydia Languish	Bob Acres
	The Sea of Ice		
	Taming a Tartar		
	Damon and Pythias	Calanthe	
	Richard III	The Queen	
	Don Caesar de Bazan	Martina	
1855	Uncle Tom's Cabin	Topsy	Phineas
	The Hundred Pound Note	(The Lady (The Peasant Girl	
	Leap Year or Lady's Privilege		

Representative Parts Taken by the Chapmans, (Cont.)

Date	Play	Role	
		Caroline Chapman	William B. Chapman
1856	A Trip to Australia or Lola Montez on the Fanny Major Richard III	Lola Montez	Tommy
1857	Delicate Ground The Dumb Belle		Alphonso O'Smirk
1861	Death or The Angel of Midnight	Angel of Midnight	
1866	The Elves		

THE CHAPMANS

BIBLIOGRAPHY

Rourke, Constance. Troupers of the Gold Coast or The Rise of
Lotta Crabtree (New York, Harcourt,Brace and Company,1928).
pp. 38-46, 49-55, 68-69, 70-71, 80-81, 112-118, 126-127,
152, 228.

Hornblow, Austin A History of the Theatre in America (Philadelphia, J. B. Lippincott, 1919). Vol. 1 p. 138.

Coad, Oral Sumner, & Mims, Edwin Jr., Pageant of America (New
Haven, Yale University Press, 1929) Vol. 14, "The American
Stage" pp. 152, 187.

Nobles, Milton. Shop Talk (Milwaukee, Riverside Printing
Co., 1881).

Smith, Sol F. Theatrical Management in the West and South
for Thirty Years (New York, Harper & Bros., 1868). Chap. 9
p. 89.

Brown, T. Allston History of the American Stage (New York,
Dick and Fitzgerald, 1870). pp. 66, 69.

Odell, George C. D. Annals of the New York Stage (New York,
Columbia University Press) Vol. V p. 220, Vol. VI pp. 56,
57, 71, 146.

McCabe, John H. Journal (San Francisco, unpublished Mss.
bound, State Library, Sutro Branch).

NEWSPAPERS AND PERIODICALS

California Historical Society Quarterly	(San Francisco,1928. Souvenirs of an Interesting Family by Helen Throop Pratt). Vol. VII pp. 282 et seq.
The Argonaut	(San Francisco), Jan. 26, 1854.
San Francisco Examiner	(American Weekly Section. March 20, 1938). p. 18
California or Daily Courier	(Published by James M.Crane, San Francisco,from January to December 1851). Oct.22-24, 28-31, Nov. 1-8,1851.

NEWSPAPERS AND PERIODICALS (Cont.)

Daily Alta California — (San Francisco). March 16, 24, April 2, 10-12, May 4-8, 12, 13, 18, June 13-15, July 12, 23, 31, Aug. 14, 1852; April 3, 17, 26, May 5, 23, June 25, July 11, Dec. 6, 7, 1853; Feb. 4-6, July 1, 11, 12, 17, 19, 24, 26, 30, 1854; Oct. 14,1867; May 9, 1876; March 3, 1880.

The San Francisco Herald — April 6, 21-25, June 12,15, 16, 19, 22, 26, 27, 29,July 1, 10, 11, 14, 31, Aug. 31, Sept. 2, 15, 19, 21, Dec.7, 1855; Sept. 1, 3, 1856;Nov. 9, 10, 11, 25, 1857.

The Golden Era — (San Francisco Public Library, Sutro Branch) Dec. 19, 1852; Jan. 2, 13, Feb. 13, 20, 27, May 22, 29, June 5, 12, 19, 26, July 3, 10, Aug. 14, 21, Sept. 18, Oct. 9, 30, 1853.

The Evening Bulletin — (San Francisco). Sept.2, 5, 24, Nov. 28, 1856; Nov. 9, 1857; Jan. 7, May 20-29, Aug. 30, 1858; April 4, 1859; Dec. 23, 1861; Jan. 22, 1866; Aug. 30, 1870; Nov. 16, 1876; March 2, 1880.

Figaro — (San Francisco). June 1, 1872.

- - - - -

PROJECT EDITORIAL STAFF

Research Director.....Jack W. Wilson

MONOGRAPH WRITERS

George Ducasse   Alan Harrison
Cornel Lengyol   Eddie Shimano

RESEARCH ASSISTANTS

Mathew Cately   Gretchen Clark
Dorothy Phillips   Lenore Legere
Lauretta Bauss   Florence Bradley
           Wyland Stanley

ART and PHOTO REPRODUCTION

Lala Eve Rivol   M. H. Mc Carty

PRODUCTION

William K. Noe   Elleanore Staschen
           Clara Mohr

Although the entire research and sten-
ographic staff on the project assisted
in the preparation of these monographs
at various stages in production, particular credit should be given to Mr.
George Ducasse for his rewrite work on
all three of the monographs in this
volume.

                    Lawrence Estevan
                    Project Supervisor.